Who Do You Say That I Am?

A Deacon's Perspective of the Diaconate

Deacon Nicholas J. La Duca, Jr.

To my wife Dorothy, the true deacon
in the La Duca family.

Contents

Ordained a Deacon – Permanently

Deacon Emil Myskowski – December, 2018

Ordained to Serve

Ordained in a manner that is permanent and clear;
a calling within a vocation – not a job nor a career.

"Ordained to Serve the people I love,"
the Lord says to us from beneath and above,
from the front and the back, left side and right;
Ordained to Serve in bright day or dark night.

We are, in effect, with each person we meet
His eyes, His ears, His heart, His hands, His feet.
Ordained to Serve in ecclesial obedience –
not with some personal or political expedience.

We each have been given specific, unique talents
to forge diaconal communities clearly that balance
correctness of doctrine with *in situ* creative insight
to heal people hurting and calm when there's fright.

Ordained to Serve in prayer and in preaching,
vested for Sacrament or by example teaching
the laity how to live out their baptismal charism
by doing what is right and just for the Lord is risen
from the dead and ascended to victory in heaven
such that His ordained deacons may humbly be leaven
in the world often unappreciated and unseen
mingling with shepherds and sheep and all in between.

Ordained to be stripped to the true self,
nailed to the cross of the Christ,
permanently steadfast and true.

As suffering strips away every form of deceit,
the deacon has nail wounds in wrists and feet.

In the streets and homes, we serve the most and the least.
In liturgies at the altar we serve at the side of the priest.

Acknowledgments

I would like to offer deep appreciation to those people who have been an encouragement to me as I have undertaken this effort. To Deacon Sam Taub, rest his soul, whom I met some 40 years ago for the first time and became my big brother, mentor, counselor, consoler, and, yes, more often than not my "corrector" (a task he was never shy nor reluctant to undertake, always to my benefit). His experiences with the then Bishop's Committee on the Diaconate, representing English-speaking deacons at conferences held in Rome, in welcoming Saint John Paul II to Detroit, as well as being an advisor to both our diaconal community, and our bishop, gave him a unique insight into the diaconate, not only from a diocesan wide, but also nationwide and worldwide perspectives. He had an insight that allowed him to patiently council me: "Nickie what you see from your limited perspective is **not** the diakonia that exists in the Church." Until the day he ended his earthly diakonia, I continually pestered him to put down in writing his experiences of the diaconate for those who come after us. Unfortunately, he never did. But as he felt his end approaching, he turned the tables and said, "Nickie, you write it." I fully expect that when we meet again, I will find him waiting with my "no holds barred" evaluation.

To Deacon Emil Myskowski, who found himself with the unenviable task of continuing to keep me "on track," which has also proven most beneficial for me, thank you. His spiritual and pastoral approach to not only his vocation as a deacon, but to all facets of life, has been a beacon for me in my diaconal vocation. As an accomplished singer, writer, and poet, he has graciously taken the time to create the poem that serves as my prologue, for which I will be forever indebted.

I also want to thank Father Dick DeLillo, OSFS, who came into my life as I was in formation and honored me by vesting me at my ordination. His instruction and counseling over the many years he walked with me on my journey, but more importantly the way he lived his vocation, introduced me to Salesian spirituality, one that gave me the encouragement to accept the fact that the way to effective diakonia was to be who I was and to be that well.

I also want to acknowledge Bishop Paul Loverde, who inherited what may be described as an "inactive" deacon community. When asked what he was going to do about it, he replied in his humble but straightforward way, "If you trust me, you will be pleased with what you see." The fruits of that promise are evident every day in those deacons he (and now his successor) has ordained, once again creating a vibrant, proactive, and productive diakonia.

Finally, to Our Lady, whose advice to deacons today remains the same, the same advice she as she once gave to those servants (i.e., diakonia) at Cana: "Do whatever He tells you."

Introduction

Forty years ago, when I was studying to become a deacon, I was challenged to write a paper on a specific topic regarding sacramental theology. In undertaking that effort, I chose to focus on the sacramental nature of the Order of Deacons because I thought this would be an easy topic to research. In truth, it proved to be more difficult than I ever would have imagined. What I did discover, however, was that the available references[1] proved to be less than satisfactory in dealing with

---

[1] Of all the references cited in the selected bibliography, there are three I feel are to be read for an overall understanding of the topic. The first, is the International Theological Commission's **"From the Diakonia of Christ to the Diakonia of the Apostles"**, a very thorough "walkthrough" of its origins, growth, and decline, particularly chapters 6 (on the reality of the diaconate today) and 7 (on the theological approach to the diaconate in the wake of Vatican II). The second is a book brought to my attention by a deacon who read the book when it was a requirement for his formation program.

the issue of who, exactly, a deacon is. More importantly, I discovered there was little information addressing the legitimate need for a distinct and permanent order of deacons. I found nothing in my research that addressed the specific concern of the meaning, value, and essence of the diaconate as not only a valid vocation, but also as an essential means of carrying out the Lord's mandate of serving others as He came to serve us. This lack of resources still exists today.

This book is the result of my quest to give adequate insight into the essence of who a deacon is. Its focus and contents are the results of my personal journey, one, I must confess, which took many turns, ran into many obstacles, had many reversals, and caused many retreats from the effort. In 2018, I attended the Deacon Congress in New Orleans, where deacons from

---

It gives a very pastoral and practical understanding of the diaconate for both those who are called to the order and those who are impacted by the presence of a deacon in their lives: **Compendium on the Diaconate**, *A Resource for the Formation, Ministry, and Life of Permanent Deacons*. The third, which I believe is a must for all deacons, deacon candidates, and those who are involved in the diaconate, whether in its establishment, its formation, its direction, or its practice, is Bishop W. Shawn McKnight's *Understanding the Diaconate*, particularly part 4, where he looks at the diaconate today in terms of the deacon's role in the liturgy (chapter 7), his ministry (chapter 8) and on restructuring the diaconate (in chapter 9).

around the United States and abroad gathered to celebrate the fiftieth anniversary of the restoration of the diaconate to its proper and permanent place in the hierarchy of the Sacrament of Holy Orders. That is a significant milestone, as well as a challenge. It is a milestone in that the seed planted at the Second Vatican Council, which came to fruition through the Moto Proprio *"Sacrum Diaconatus Ordinem"* of Pope Saint Paul VI, has grown worldwide and is now universally recognized as a reality. Yet it also revealed a continuing challenge: how to proclaim the reality in a way that makes manifest not merely **what** a deacon is, but **who** a deacon is. Because to understand who the deacon is, one must recognize, as Collins points out[2], that "diakonia is used as [not only] a description of Jesus' life work" but also (in quoting Brant[3]) to "express the meaning of His life," in short, to express **who he was.** Now why is that not only a challenge, but a critical challenge, even an **essential** challenge? Then and only then by focusing on *who* a deacon is can we truly discover **what** not only the Church, but Our Lord, is asking of His deacons in serving His sheep.

---

[2] John Collins, *Deacons and the Church*, Gracewing, Morehouse Publishing, Harrisburg, PA, pg. 49.

[3] Brant, Dienst und Dienen in Neuen Testament (Gutersloh 1931, pg. 70).

"It is because, as Aquinas notes, action (what something does) reflects nature/personhood (what or who a thing is). And it is only once we can get to the essence or personhood of the diaconate that we can begin to understand why the Church restored the diaconate as a Personal Vocation and thus to its proper and permanent place in its hierarchy."

In beginning to develop the content of the book, I found it was turning out to be a theoretical rather than an experiential endeavor. Experiences gained both positive, in terms of the ministries I have been blessed to work in, as well as negative, in the reception by which the validity of my vocation as a deacon was received.

So, after what I would describe as a deep, yet uncomfortable period of prayer and discernment, I came to what I felt was the answer. The answer coming to me in my experiences gained from the Deacon Congress held in New Orleans. Not to focus on the Order of Deacon from the perspective of *what* it was by mandate the Order was restored to do (or not do), but the essence of *who* a deacon is, regardless of what he could or couldn't do at any particular time in the life of the Church. My objective is to inform the reader of the validity of the restored diaconate as a true and essential part of the Sacrament of Holy Orders. I am committed to presenting the diaconate in terms of who the deacon is in the hierarchy of the Catholic Church.

Because in both the events and experiences leading up to its restoration, the focus of both the Church, theologians, and laity has been primarily (if not exclusively) on determining what a deacon should/could do or not do. Whether liturgically, pastorally, or in proclaiming the teachings of the Church, the focus has been primarily historical: should these "restored" deacons do what deacons did in the apostolic Church, the patristic Church, the medieval Church, or the Church of Trent? Or should the focus be on what the Church in the modern world calls for in terms of the ministerial deacon, even if that is distinct from, or even different than, what deacons did or did not do in the past? For it is my contention that to focus on what the deacon did or did not do or what the deacon is presently tasked with doing will create what I would describe as the "Brer Rabbit" syndrome. Where, like Brer Rabbit and his attempts to "get to know the Tar Baby," the more we attempt to delve into the specifics of what a deacon can/ought do or not to do, the more we, like Brer Rabbit, will find ourselves bogged down in the "accidents" or externals of what a deacon does. In following these efforts, we will find ourselves like Brer Rabbit: stymied, at least frustrated, in coming to grips with who the deacon is. More importantly, we will distract ourselves in coming to an understanding of why it was that Our Lord established the Sacrament of Holy Orders, a sacrament whose purpose He chose to demonstrate by His actions, both during and after the Last Supper. Actions which He shared in the upper room with His apostles, upon whom the sacrament was to be first confected. Actions that would reveal His mandate to those who would receive that sacrament to offer to His Church both sacrifice (through those ordained to the priesthood) and service (through those ordained to the Order of Deacon).

Taking this approach, it is my hope that the reader will better understand **who** the deacon is in the Church's hierarchy. This will increase our understanding of the Sacrament of Holy Orders, particularly as it relates to the Order of Deacon. And this will enlighten us as to why it was that the fathers of Vatican Council II (VC II), in the council's third session opted to "duly vote for the restoration of a ministry called diaconate"[4] and why they determined that the time was right for restoring the Order of Deacon to its proper and traditional place in the hierarchy of Holy Orders.

In a nutshell, this is what this book is all about: my attempt

---

[4] Collins, *Deacons and the Church,* pg. 43. For a more in depth understanding of what took place at the council regarding the diaconate, one of the better sources would be chapter 9 in Deacon William Ditewig's book *The Emerging Diaconate, Servant Leaders in a Servant Church*, Paulist Press, New York/Mahwah, NJ, 2007.

in and through both formal and informal experiences over the last thirty-five years, both personally and through my interactions with my brother deacons from a number of dioceses in the United States, to provide an answer to the question: "Who is a deacon?" I am confident that any progress this effort may contribute to answering that question will help the Church as to who the deacon is in terms of his vocation, his place, and his function.

In attempting to achieve this objective, I begin chapter 1 by explaining why it is the case we need to focus on who the deacon is in order to clearly recognize both the necessity for and validity of a restored diaconate to its proper and permanent place in the Church's hierarchy. This leads to a discussion in chapter two regarding the validity of the restored diaconate as a true vocation. Then in chapter three, I look at its effectiveness in terms of fulfilling the objectives for which it was restored, through a synergistic and cooperative relationship with both the bishop and the priest. In chapter four, I focus on addressing a diakonia that can only be effective by understanding the essence of that service. Although recognizing we have come a long way in the fifty years the Latin Church has experienced the restored diaconate, there are still challenges that need to be addressed. I try to address the reality of some of those challenges to the diaconate in chapter five.

Chapter 1
The Who *Not* the What

It has been fifty years since Vatican Council II, and the Church is still assimilating the teachings of the council into its practices. As a result, several of these teachings are still unclear to many Catholics. One of these teachings concerns the restoration of the Order of Deacon to its proper and permanent place in the hierarchy of the Sacrament of Holy Orders. Now, I, after some thirty-five years since being called to serve both Jesus and His people as a deacon, have come to an understanding of why there is still confusion about the deacon. The confusion has, as pointed out by Plater,[5] "caused [intentionally as well as unintentionally, I might add] controversy, debate, and resistance in some places" as to not only what defines a deacon or why, but also what needs, if any, exist for deacons. And in

---

[5] Osmonde Plater, *Many Servants: An Introduction to Deacons*, Cowley Publications, Boston, MA, pgs. 2-3.

reflecting on that reality, I have found that the reason is that the focus of the many honest, intellectual, determined efforts both within the Church and outside is on what a deacon is rather than who a deacon is. This is a focus that I have found whether the diaconate is looked at from a theological, ecclesiastical, or historical perspective.

Therefore, in this chapter I will briefly look at how the diaconate has developed after Vatican II and challenges which have arisen from this development. I will look at the "common way" as well as the "better way" to view the deacon from the Vatican II lens. Then I will look at the challenge of the deacon and priest pertaining to occupation and vocation. Finally, I will draw some conclusions based on these challenges as to how we can move forward defining the deacon.

Deacon and Vatican II-Common vs Better Way

With the promulgation by Saint Pope Paul VI of his Apostolic Letter ***Sacrum Diaconatus Ordinem*** on June 18, 1967, there has been an increased interest within the Church when it comes to the Order of Deacon. This is an interest that has been of benefit to making present to the world the reality of the restored Order of Deacon and that has been seen in an increasing number of books, documents, and articles written on the diaconate[6]. The overall result, however, has raised as many questions as they have answers. A proliferation of sources which, while devoted to the diaconate has added—rather than clarify—to the confusion as to who the deacon is. What is the reason for this?

This has caused me to ask, why is that? I posit the reason is that those many efforts, albeit generally with "good intentions" to recognize and attempt to explain this "modern presence" of deacons in the Church, have not taken the "better way." A way that will enable one to focus on the essence of who the deacon is in terms of the ontological reason for the deacon's presence. Yet, rather than taking such an approach, I find the efforts to take what I would call the more common way, a way that looks at what a deacon is or is not or what he can or cannot do in terms of the tangible limits of his faculties relating to the word, liturgy, or service.

The apostles we find, learned, as did their successors at VC II, there was a need to distribute the activities associated with doing Christ's will among those He set aside to do so. This is true whether they be bishops who continue to lead His sheep by holding fast to the Deposit of Faith, priests to continue to

---

[6] For an example, see the Selected Bibliography, particularly the book by Bishop McKnight, which was noted earlier and is based on his doctoral dissertation on the diaconate.

feed His sheep, *or* deacons to continue to serve His sheep. Yet in the Latin Church, there is a focus on *what* each was distinctly called to do in carrying out that mandate rather than *who it was and why it was* that the Lord chose to call specific men to the distinct orders of bishop, priest, or deacon.

By better understanding the council's decision, I believe meaningful progress can be made in terms of making a healthy integration of the restored diaconate as a permanent and not merely transitional presence in the life of the Church a reality. Doing so will enable the role, functioning, and relationship of the distinct grades of the Sacrament of Holy Orders not only to be recognized, but be realized. And it is important that we can recognize the truth of the premise that the Deposit of Faith, the content of which was completed with the death of the last apostle, continues under the direction of the magisterium, as guided by the Holy Spirit and to grow in the understanding and applicability of the diaconate. Therefore, why would it not be appropriate to say that the diaconate, an office at least of apostolic origin, cannot also continue to grow in terms of its understanding and, more importantly, in its the applicability of that office to the Church's mission?

A question of particular importance regarding the deacon is as follows: Who among the ordained clergy is directly challenged in making Christ the Servant, the first deacon, present to His Church? Is it not the deacon, by the way he is called to live his vocation, who not only enables Christ to be the one recognized, but more importantly experienced? This is the case whether in terms of the Word preached or assisting at the altar, from which emanates the source by which and the summit to which all Christian service is empowered, or in serving all those who bear His image and to whom He mandated we recognize by that service. By his ordination, it is the deacon.

Yet one of the key impediments to a proper and realistic understanding of the diaconate in the Church is the (maybe mistaken?) idea that most people have about the diaconate: the diaconal ministry is linked primarily in some way to the formal functioning of the institutional Church, that is, the cathedral or the parish building, or to the formal functioning that takes place within the Church, for example, the RCIA program, sacramental preparation, or liturgical activities. Then, when Catholics learn of the fact that (most) deacons hold down secular or civilian jobs and, thus, are not normally physically present on the cathedral or parish premises, they tend to look at deacons as being "part-time" clergy. This comes as a result of comparing deacons with priests, who are perceived as "full-time" clergy. A perception which causes, in terms of a "vocation," deacons (as opposed to priests) as being looked at as either not having a vocation, or at best, having an avocation. This is a perception, unfortunately, after a half century, that is not limited to the laity, but one that is also held by some priests (and, sadly, I must confess, by some deacons, as well).

Deacon vs. Priest—Pertaining to Occupation and Vocation

This brings us to the second challenge of understanding the diaconate after Vatican II. Most men ordained to the Order of Deacon are married. And although there is no lack of literature on the celibate lifestyle as it relates to the Sacrament of Holy Orders, there is little, if any, literature relating to the married lifestyle (albeit, in the Latin Church, limited to the Order of Deacon). This further adds to the confusion as to whether the deacon has a vocation when compared with that of the priest.

I am convinced that this confusion comes about because of the way many look at the commitment a man makes in entering Holy Orders (priesthood) and the commitment to do so by living a celibate life, which many see (from a negative worldview) as a "sacrifice." This sacrifice involves "giving up" the ability to enter into an intimate relationship with a woman. In my opinion, from that narrow understanding of the commitment to celibacy that is associated with the priesthood, one can reasonably apply that "logic" to a man entering into the Sacrament of Marriage and say he is doing something similar. Isn't he also voluntarily "sacrificing" his ability to enter into an intimate relationship with any other woman than the woman he sacramentally commits to be with for life?

However, in gaining a true understanding of the beauty and purpose of celibacy, one must look at the "sacrifice" to either commit to celibacy or matrimony as ***not*** a "giving up" but rather as a giving *of* oneself exclusively to another. In the case of the celibate to Christ and the married man to his wife. Only by focusing on the other-centered nature of both ways of life can we then truly make progress in focusing on the similarity in the giving of both to their commitment to the Sacrament of Holy Orders—whether as a priest sacramentally committed to a life of celibacy or a deacon sacramentally committed to a married life—rather than the worldly perspectives of the difference between the two ways of life.

Let us return to the perception that a deacon is "only" a deacon when at "church." This defies credibility. To make my point, one needs only to look at a man (or woman) who has received the Sacrament of Matrimony. Would one say that as a result of their work that forces them to spend more time away from their home (and spouse) that they are "part-time" spouses? So although not at home, would we say they are not married persons? Absurd! All would recognize that a married person, by virtue of their free and willing acceptance of not only the sacramental covenant they entered, but also their commitment to live that commitment, was doing so not on a part-time basis, but on a full, permanent, and unconditional basis. Why then, when one stops and thinks about it, would it be any different for a man, whether married or not, to have that same commitment, that same obligation to his call, his vocation to the Sacrament of Holy Orders, which he freely and willingly enters into at his ordination to the diaconate?

This is a misperception influenced in the Western Church by the fact that for the last millennium, the Order of Deacon has been looked at not as a permanent way of ministry, but as a transition between the lay state and priesthood. This misperception from both ecclesiastical practice and canonical discipline can be allowed to exist by the Church's authority, as pointed out by Cardinal Gerhard Muller. He does go on, however, to also point out that there is no basis for this (mis)perception from a sacramental theology perspective.[7] Although the diaconate has always been an integral part of the Church's hierarchy, an effective theology of the diaconate,

____

[7] Gerhard Muller, *Priesthood and Diaconate*, Ignatius Press, San Francisco, pgs. 53-54.

particularly regarding a proper responsive presence of Christ the servant to that Church, has yet to be developed. So when we look at the reality of a renewed concept of diakonia as a valid and proper way of ministry, we need to understand why its permanence was restored by the fathers of VCII with the approval of Pope Saint Paul VI.

However, it should be noted that while looking at the past, whether it be the writings of Paul; the numerous apostolic fathers and patristic theologians; or the fruits of the many councils that have addressed the diaconate leading up to VCII, one must be aware of two things. First, the Church is a living, learning body, not a static organization, and its effectiveness is directly related to its ability to apply the Lord's message of love and service timely and relevantly to the cultural environment in which it exists. Second, although one would be foolish to ignore the past, one would be even more foolish to stay in it.

Therefore, I posit that the primary idea pertaining to the deacon having a permanent presence in the Church's hierarchy is that of a Servant Church. If we are a servant Church and if as Saint Pope Paul VI notes, "The Church exists in order to evangelize" (*Evangelii nuntiandi*#14)—that is, to put itself at the service of the Gospel and to bring that gift to others—then it makes sense to have an order to remind us of the essential meaning of the Church. This is not only in heavenly terms, which equates to the actions of Christ in and through the sacraments, but in worldly terms, which equates to the social dimensions of service, as might clearly be evidenced in the corporal and spiritual works of mercy, to which we find that Christ's public ministry was oriented.

This reality is made present in the deacon, who participates primarily in assisting the bishop and his priests by providing sacramental service to Christ's people. His primary value in serving the Lord is not to be found in the building of the Church (e.g., assisting at mass, presiding at a baptism, or blessing a wedding couple), but in the workplace, the marketplace, and the community in which he lives while pursuing his chosen profession (whether that profession be a prominent one or a humble one). This is the environment in which he is committed to living his diaconal vocation. This is a way in which he can lead others to want to know and follow Jesus; it is a commitment that enables the "human race [to] become the family of God, in which love would be the fulfillment of the law" (Gaudium et Spes #32).

An orientation that enables the essential role of a deacon in the Church and the world in which the Church exists to be recognized as distinct from that of a priest. This enables one to better understand that the Church's mandate in the world, which is to serve believers and nonbelievers alike through all its baptized, does so in a singular way for those ordained as deacons, who strengthened by sacramental grace. A mandate which deacons do uniquely by living out their sacramental vocation and their secular profession in a transparent way. By doing so, deacons show both believers and nonbelievers" (cf Gaudium et Spes # 21) that living the message of love is not only doable, but fruitful.

The Church, then, given this mandate, poses the following question: Which vocation can better do so? The priest, who normally lives his vocation "rectory based," or the deacon, who normally lives his vocation "community based?"

This is important in understanding the essential role of a deacon in the Church and the world in which the Church exists. The Church through all its baptized, but in a singular way for those ordained as deacons, is strengthened by sacramental grace to serve both believers and nonbelievers alike. Deacons do this by living out their sacramental vocation but also their secular profession in a transparent way.

In conclusion, by focusing on what a deacon is or does creates a dissonance evident in today's Church as to who the deacon is. This is true not only in terms of his vocation, but also in his place in the Church and his relationship to both other clergy and the laity. This is a point that has been brought home to me in an unexpected experience in the sacristy of Saint

Peter's in Rome, where having had the honor of assisting at the Sunday liturgy and while divesting after Mass, I had several priests from various European countries come up to me and found it fascinating to be able to ask who I, a permanent deacon, was and what I was all about. They asked about the advantages and disadvantages of being married and serving the Church as an ordained minister or how I was received by both the priests and the laity to whom I ministered. And in that experience, it dawned on me that while the Church has come to recognize and accept the validity of the deacon's ecclesiastical status, it has yet to fully recognize (and maybe accept) its ecclesiastical identity.

This is a circumstance that explains why the deacon (too) often is confronted with the following question: "Who are you?" This is a critical question that needs to be answered not only by deacons, but all who not only desire to serve Christ and live like Christ. This is the same question, Jesus, the first deacon, asked of His apostles: not **what** others or they thought He was, but **who** He was. Why? Because by limiting their focus on what He was—redeemer, savior, forgiver, healer, which He truly was and is—they would lose sight of the reason why He was able to be so, because of who He was: The Son of God made man. In short, one would say His effectiveness (what He did) was the result of His essence (who He was).

The same challenge faces us today: coming up with the answer to the question who (the Church, the world, etc.) believes the deacon is. Who is the person that was at VCII, in Lumen Gentium: #29, determined to be restored *"as a proper and stable* (italics added) rank of the hierarchy?"[8] Therefore, it is essential that the question "deacon, who are you?" must not only be addressed but answered.

Thus, it is essential that a proper understanding of who the deacon is be made. This is an understanding without which the many efforts to properly "place" the deacon not only within the hierarchy of the Church's clergy, but more importantly within the body of the Church, its people, will continue to produce not only confusion among those with whom the deacon interacts and will not be fruitful. The result of which will continue to the frustration as to who the deacon is, as not only exhibited within the Church and the laity, but within the diaconate itself. More importantly, without an understanding of who a deacon is—and thus what is the proper role for deacons in the Church—I contend that the proper understanding of the Sacrament of Holy Orders held by the

---

[8] Which Osborne points out in his book *The Permanent Diaconate, Its History, and Place in the Sacraments of Orders,* Paulist Press, New York/Mahwah NJ, pg. 7 as being one of the five major conciliar changes in the church's understanding of ministry.

apostolic fathers and the patristic theologians will be corrupted at the least and contradicted at the worst[9].

The key, then, is not the why but the intent of the fathers of VCII in restoring the diaconate to its proper place in the hierarchy of Holy Orders. This is a point made interesting by the comment of one presenter at the recent deacon congress held to celebrate the fiftieth anniversary of the diaconate: "the council restored the diaconate not because of a lack of priests, but because of a ***lack of deacons***" (emphasis added). This is a point I am in total agreement with. For if (God willing) there is a tenfold increase in the number of vocations to the priesthood, there will still be (by virtue of the distinction in both vocations and where and how the two vocations are lived) a need (I would go so far to say a necessity) for deacons. Therefore, if we, as deacons, are to heed the call by Pope Francis

---

[9] This is the case because the focus has been—and unfortunately still is on—what a deacon can or cannot do, rather than who the deacon is and why he was ordained by Our Lord at the Last Supper to be an integral part of the Sacrament of Orders He chose to institute at that time. This is a point that Osborne notes (pgs. 143-145) has been a challenge that has existed from the earliest days of the church, noting that the diaconal ministry was very diverse then (and now, I might add) and was in "constant change and development" (which I believe, if it is to be what the council fathers envisioned it to be, will continue to do so).

to go where the Church, as represented by her ordained ministers, cannot only "smell the sheep," but feel the sheep, one thing is essential: that deacons work side by side with those called to the episcopate and priesthood in tending to those sheep.[10] This is a task that is even more essential in the environment in which the Church finds itself today, given the fact the deacon normally lives his vocation in such an environment, hence making the presence of the diaconate not only necessary, but essential.

Therefore, in looking at the Order of Deacon, if any meaningful progress can or even will be made in terms of a healthy and effective integration of the restored diaconate as a permanent and not merely transitional presence in the life of the Church, an understanding of who the deacon is becomes essential. Having this will enable us to understand the apostolic practice as to the role and functioning of the three distinct grades of the Sacrament of Holy Orders. Interestingly (after an albeit cursory review of a selection of their writings), I found no evidence of the Order of Deacon being merely a means of transitioning to the priesthood.[11]

---

[10] Pope Francis at the March 28, 2013 Chrism Mass, Saint Peter's Basilica.

[11] A point made by Osborne in pointing out that there is "no historical data indicating that there was an official edict revoking the

Thus, this is a mandate of Jesus, the first deacon, when He established His Church, at which was to proclaim His message and reveal the presence of His Kingdom and to serve others as He did so perfectly. This is a mandate He gave His disciples at the Last Supper, in the washing of their feet. It is an action summed up so perfectly in His public ministry by which He served His Father in doing the same for others. This is a mandate He gave His disciples, along with the perpetuation of His perfect sacrifice, which was to serve others as He had served them but to do each in a unique and sacramental way. Some were asked to perpetuate His most perfect sacrifice through their vocation to the priesthood. Others were asked to continue His serving of His people, wherever they may be found, whether inside or outside the Church through their vocation to the diaconate, one that begins by first serving at His altar, from which emanates the source and summit of all that is necessary for the deacon to encourage those served wherever His ministry takes Him, to truly recognize Christ's presence in their lives.

---

permanent diaconate" and that the "(permanent) diaconal ministry from AD 800 onward became the exception and eventually disappeared." Osborne, *The Permanent Diaconate*. 94. Although Barnett, in his book *The Diaconate, A Full and Equal Order* gives a possible reason to be the development of *cursus honorum* than from any other single factor (pg. 106).

Chapter 2

Vocation ... "vocation" ... "avocation"

One of the challenges in any attempt at understanding who the deacon is revolves around the implicit but evident confusion among both clergy and laity as to whether a deacon has a true vocation or merely, at best, an avocation. What "fuels" this discussion is that almost all of those men who have not only heard the call but responded to that call, with the approval of the Holy Spirit and the concurrence of the ordaining bishop, are or have been in a civilian, government, or military career before or at the time of their ordination. A point brought home to me in a discussion with a priest I respect who told me that those men called to the diaconate were really responding to a "second call," whereas those called to the priesthood or consecrated life[12] were responding to a "first call. "If so, the

---

[12] A perception that Echlin (*The Deacon and the Church, Past and Future*) points out is this at best a mistaken one because he notes that

question one would then ask is, would that same criteria apply to those men, who after a successful secular career, or marriage (in the case of a widower) discern their call to the priesthood and become ordained priests?

This is a perception I believe requires us to look a little closer at this concept of "vocation." For if the diaconate is to be truly recognized as a legitimate vocation, then one would reasonably expect the identification, screening, and selecting of men for Holy Orders, whether to the priesthood or diaconate, be a direct concern of the diocesan office of vocations—which generally is not the case. We must then ask why. Vatican Council II recognized the call to the Order of Deacon is for men, single or married, who in faith accepted the Lord's promise that He will go before them always. The key is to focus on a man's call to the diaconate as genuine, whether he is married or not. In this, discerning the legitimate call to the diaconate should welcome, or at least accept, those men who are not married with the same enthusiasm as they would married men. Unfortunately, this is not always the case.

This is an attitude that seems to imply there is a growing,

"the deacon's role is not 'lower than' nor 'inferior to' the priest, he [then deacon] is not a potential rival, his charism is **different** than any other charism in the church **including** that of the priest" (emphasis added).

albeit implicit, sense within the Church that the diaconate is limited or oriented toward married men, which further implies that for unmarried men, the "normal" path to serving the Lord is not the diaconate but the priesthood. This is an attitude, at least within the Latin Rite, where the discipline of celibacy is seen as a requisite for men to enter into the priesthood or religious life, is the basis for recognizing it as the "true" means to a vocation. This raises the following question: Is the call to the diaconate for married men recognized as a legitimate way to serve Christ and His Church by the fathers of VCII, a legitimate vocation that should have ***nothing to do with one's marital status?*** This raises yet another question regarding those unmarried men who believe they are not called to the priesthood but to the diaconate: Does their "vocation" come into question as well? Think about that for a moment. With the exception of Saint John, there is no consensus, save for a leaning to the belief that the other apostles (specifically Saint Peter), or at least a majority of them, were married. Should those who were married have their vocation looked at as a "second call" or should their vocation be questioned as well? When looked at it from the perspective of their being married, one would see the absurdity of that argument. Should that not also apply to those married men who are ordained deacons?

Christian theologians, the magisterium, and the Catechism

of the Catholic Church clearly teach that God is omniscient. With Him, there is no past or future but an eternal present. Then while in His human nature, and later through the Person of the Holy Spirit, why would He not only choose to call and allow married men to serve Him as **both** priests and deacons? This is a practice we find being the custom in the Latin Church for almost the first millennium of His Church's existence. The "argument "that has been proposed by some to deal with this issue is that those men who were married left their wives to follow their vocation, whether as priests or deacons. This leaves (at least for me) a lot of questions. Could an omniscient God have been mistaken when He stated that what He had joined together (i.e., in the covenant or Sacrament of Marriage) no one(person) could put asunder? Would God, being a personal and loving God, who both priests and deacons are called to serve, have changed His mind? Remember the Lord's admonition to those who challenged Him regarding the prevalent practice of divorce? This would mean that our loving God would renege on His commitment to His first covenantal command and rend asunder a valid marriage, a valid vocation.[13]

---

[13] Particularly when looking at the marriage covenant between a man and a woman as foremost a covenant of love, Collins points out, "'Diakonia' was the manifestation of love and…would not be truly manifested in the church until it was embodied in an independent

Looking then at the question of vocation, one needs to delve a little deeper to come to an understanding of the concept of vocation. Looking, for example, at the definition of vocation found in the Catholic Dictionary,[14] we find it as "a call from God to a distinct state of life, in which a person can reach holiness." It then goes on to state, "The Second Vatican Council made it plain that there is "a universal [vocation] to holiness in the Church," (see Lumen Gentium 39). So just what does having a "vocation" imply?

The Archdiocese of Melbourne gives some good insight into our efforts in answering that question. It states, "A vocation is more than an ordinary call…it is not the same as your career or profession…A career or a profession [it goes on to point out] is something that you have to support yourself and contribute in some way to the good of society." It then goes on to stress there is quite a significant distinction between a career/profession and a vocation by pointing out that one "can pick, choose, and switch professions freely, depending on [one's] preferences…or circumstances." What I find to be most significant is where it

---

ecclesiastical office." Put differently (as will be addressed later), what better way to experience or model love than by being in a lifelong, unconditional "state of love" best embodied in the sacramental union of a man and a woman in marriage?

[14] catholicculture.org

states that when it comes to vocation, "it is no longer what do I prefer? But rather what does God want me to be? "It then points out that "a vocation is not something that you can switch like a profession or career, "concluding with the point that "each vocation [whether it be to the single life, married life, consecrated life or the ordained ministry] is a commitment to love God in a certain way…[That] the object of every vocation is God…with its primary object [being to love God]." Thus, one could sum up an understanding of a career as being a means for enabling a person to be productive for themselves (whether in terms of professional, personal, or financial satisfaction) in a way that they contribute to the growth of society and the economy. This differentiates it from a vocation, which is a means for enabling a person to be effective in helping others (whether spouses, as in the case of those deacons who are married, or members of the congregation, as is the case in both the community and the congregation) to experience God's, love, God's mercy, and God's presence in their lives.

From my experience as a deacon, here lies the crux of the confusion, particularly as it pertains to the Order of Deacon. The reality is that the majority of men ordained in today's church are married. This recognizes that although the primary way the married deacon is called to serve is through the Sacrament of Marriage, it is not the only way he is called to serve Jesus. Further, he sees his vocation as a deacon as a member of the Church's hierarchy, by which he will do God's will in servicing others (his vocation). This is a perception not held by the deacon ordained a priest. He sees the diaconate, which he lives in a celibate state, not as a permanent but a transitory step to fulfilling his vocation by serving Him through sacrifice and absolution.

This creates one of the major "obstacles" to accepting the call to the diaconate as a genuine vocation. This is a challenge that rests with the fact that over 90% of the men who have responded to the call to serve the Lord in the Order of Deacon as a permanent ministry are married. This challenge is strengthened by Saint Paul's concern expressed in his first letter to the Corinthians (cf 7:32-38) that a married man, as opposed to the celibate man, who "cares for things that belong to the Lord," will find himself, in serving the Lord, "in conflict with his cares for things of the world," which, one would gather from inference, would be because of either his family obligations, his career obligations, or both. Yet it is interesting to note that Saint Paul goes on to point out that in his efforts to do God's work by carrying out the same mandates and commission the twelve did, he and his companions chose to do so not at the Church's expense, but by paying their own way by their laboring…night and day (2 Thess 3:8).

Put another way, one might get the mistaken impression that "caring for things of the world" would impact and even prevent a man from dutifully "caring about things of the Lord. "This is a position that is an absurd, yet sadly, a prevalent opinion still held by both the laity and clergy. Indeed, some believe the deacon, because of his marital status and the concomitant requirement to earn a livelihood in the secular workplace (as, by the way, Paul himself chose to do), is merely a "part time clergyman. Thus, a deacon is considered as not having a "full-time" (i.e., "real") vocation serving the Lord through the Sacrament of Holy Orders when compared with a "full-time" priest. This is a perception evidenced by a priest, for example, telling a deacon: "I don't know when you are available. "This is a perception that can be attributed to both the deacon and the priest, which I discuss in greater detail below on priest–deacon relationships. One can also look at it from the perception of a parishioner in asking the deacon how being a deacon "part time" at the parish affects his work schedule. If thought about, this would imply that the deacon leaves his (hypothetical) collar at the metro station or parking lot on his way to work. Using that same rationale, would one ask if the married man leaves his wedding ring alongside it? The later, obviously, from the perspective of both the priest and parishioner, is ridiculous. Why then does not the same perception hold true of the diaconal vocation?

Now, how does one address this challenge? First, we can ask the following question: Can a man be called to more than one vocation? This is important when recognizing that some men (or women) can and are called by the Lord to carry out His Father's mandate to "become one and multiply" by living that call in the covenantal bond of marriage, raised by the Lord to a sacramental vocation. At the same time, however, one must also recognize that that the Lord can and has called some men to serve His Father, acting in His person through the Sacrament of Holy Orders. The question that arises is the following: Has the Lord chosen to limit His call to men to only **one path** of vocation, the married state **or** the clerical state? And what makes the question more complex, at least from the perspective of the Latin Rite (in contrast to the Eastern rites and the Orthodox Church, which both possess valid sacraments), is to infer by its tradition for the past thousand years that the call to the clerical state is limited to a single or celibate lifestyle.

Or can the Lord, in His unlimited freedom, choose to call some men to serve Him through and in **both** vocations? Saint Paul goes on to point out in that same pericope cited earlier: "*marriage is **not** inferior to singleness in any way,* "and both the single (celibate) and married man must make sure they "attend to the Lord without distraction" (cf 7:35).

Thus, the question is not whether there is one vocation or two, for historically, theologically, and scripturally (cf Paul to Timothy), married men have been called to serve the Lord in all three grades of the Sacrament of Holy Orders, beginning with the call to the twelve. The question then is really whether the married state and the clerical state, particularly in the case of the Latin Rite married deacon (a question, by the way, that would be equally applicable to the vocational status of Eastern rite and Orthodox priests) are two separate or *distinct* vocations.

For if the two vocations in the case of married clergy are looked at as being *separate,* then all the arguments supporting the contention that the diaconate (at least for married men) is not, in the extreme, a "true" vocation would not be true. This is an argument that would lead to the perception that, at best, it would be a "second calling," which may have some merit, particularly in arguing that the "conflicting" priorities of the two "separate" calls is at one extreme, a definite distraction, and, at the other extreme, an almost insurmountable hurdle that must be overcome to do the Lord's work as a member of His clergy.

Yet if the two vocations are looked at as being *distinct* and **not** separate (as it is looked at by our Eastern rite and Orthodox brothers living the two vocations), then a more accurate assessment of the deacon's vocation becomes evident. For then, we can see the value of a man strengthened with the graces of ordination to the Order of Deacon (particularly in the case of the married deacon) who is living his diaconal vocation both in the world, in the workplace he can better pursue it because of those sacramental graces to bring Christ's presence to those besides whom he works and plays, but also in the Church, where he exercises his threefold ministry of liturgy, word, and service. The deacon brings the One who chose not to be served, but to serve those who come to Christ for His comfort. And this is the case whether it be for strengthening through his liturgical ministry, instruction through his ministry of the word, or acceptance through his pastoral servanthood.

In any case, what is marriage? Isn't it the institution of the domestic Church in the family, which was so often expressed by Saint John Paul II in his many writings upon which the Church is founded? It is the domestic Church, in which the married deacon unconditionally has committed to living his marital vocation. This is a vocation by which he has committed to living his marital vocation to love and to serve and respect his wedded spouse for who she is.

This is a commitment by which the deacon gains a personal and intimate experience that will guide him better serve the Church. If one stops and thinks about it from the perspective of two distinct rather than separate vocations, one can then pause and ask the following: What better experience is there for enabling a man to not only strengthen, but to Iive his threefold call to the diaconate, and his commitment to the institutional Church, here recognized as Christ's bride? Can one not see how those experiences gained within his domestic Church can only help him in living his commitment made at the reception of the Sacrament of Holy Orders to the Church.

These are experiences that will enable the married deacon, in living his liturgical commitment, to be strengthened by his marital commitment to reveal personally the experience the Lord's presence in their lives. By being able to personally do so not only can show others what one's commitment to participating in the liturgy entails, but also can show the graces the liturgy imparts to those who participate in it. Thus, in his proclaiming the word, the message of God's law of love for us, the deacon's marital experiences will better enable him to not only expose what that law of love entails, but how that love is to be experienced in and through others. Finally, through his commitment to service, his marital experiences will better enable him to demonstrate to others that true discipleship and how it involves a love-based vocation (in whatever form it may take) to and for the wellbeing of others, one that goes beyond the worldliness of ritual and the obedience to ordinances.

Yet despite the Church's fifty years of experience, in light of the growth of the diaconate, not only in the United States but worldwide, the question of vocation still lingers. Thus, if any progress is to be made in recognizing that the call to the Order of Deacon is not only an ecclesiastical reality but an ontological reality, the question of who a deacon is must not only be addressed in a direct and decisive manner, but must be answered in a definitive way that will leave no doubt or confusion as to that reality.

However, one significant challenge is still to be faced. It is to be found in the very process by which a man responds to the Lord's call to serve Him as either a priest or deacon. It is what I call the "***step process***." This is the case for **both** men who are called by Our Lord to serve Him either in offering sacrifice through the Order of Presbyterate or to offer service to Him through the Order of Deacon; these men are faced with a personal challenge to discern if that call is genuine and then to see if their faith is strong enough to say yes. Once it is determined to be a yes, they must petition their bishop who, as a successor to His apostles, is given the charisma to determine whether that man should be permitted to begin his particular and personal journey to fulfilling his answer to his Lord's call.

With the bishop saying yes, whether the call is to the priesthood or the diaconate, the man then begins his journey, which begins either by entering a seminary or a deacon formation program. From this point on, the journeys take on an identical path, albeit not necessarily in terms of immersion, but of progress.

After a period of discernment and with their bishop's approval, men aspiring to the priesthood or the diaconate take the next step and are admitted into candidacy for ordination. Again, after another period of discernment and with the bishop's approval, both men take the next step and receive the ministry of Lector. Once more, after another period of discernment, both men, are admitted into the ministry of Acolyte. Now *here* is where the seed of confusion as to the validity of the Order of Deacon as a true vocation is sown. Because after yet another period of discernment, and again with the bishop's deliberate approval, both men take the next step: ***Ordination to the Order of Deacon.***

Whereas the one man ordained a deacon as the *final* step and finds himself, as a deacon, called to serve his Lord as his permanent and deliberate way of life, thus entering into his true calling. The other man, called to serve his Lord as his priest— while also seeing his ordination to the diaconate as an ontological change in his being with the reception of the Sacrament of Holy Orders—sees it as merely the *next*, albeit, important step toward entering into his true calling: to live *not as a deacon*, but as a priest of the Order of Melchizedek.

This is the reason some, whether priest or layperson, mistakenly see only the Order of Presbyterate as the true vocation of Holy Orders. What happens when a man originally called to the priesthood, who after being ordained a deacon, finds himself hesitating to take the "next step?" What does the Church do with him, particularly after a period of discernment, during which he may come to the realization that he wishes to continue to serve his Lord not as a priest but as a deacon? Is he allowed to continue serving his Lord as a deacon, or is he laicized? With the current practice to laicize him, rather than let him continue as a deacon, what does that imply when it comes to the recognition of the diaconate as a genuine calling, particularly in the eyes of the Church, as it effects both its clergy and laity?

And thus, although much progress has been made over the last fifty years, particularly in the recognition of the reality of the presence of the diaconate in the Church, there continues to be confusion as to what that presence means. In response to a question asked of him at a meeting with parish priests and deacons of the diocese of Rome about what he thought should be the proper tasks of deacons in Rome, Benedict XVI pointed out, "[That] somewhat exceeds my capacity…I think that one characteristic of the diaconal ministry is precisely the multiplicity of its applications." This confusion still exists even in light of the reality that it is an order that can trace its origins to the age of the apostles.[15] And it is an order, that if genuinely exercised, makes present by that exercise, the Presence of the First Deacon, the Perfect Deacon, Jesus, who revealed to the world that He came not to be served by others, but to serve them. And, in His doing so, Christ taught us the best way to do so was by example.

Now, given the virtue of the circumstances a priest and deacon find themselves in when it comes to exercising their particular vocations, one must ask the following: Which of the two has the better opportunity to do so—to answer His call to serve Christ, in his people, *wherever they may be?* This is a question of such importance to the Church that it caused Saint John Paul II to challenge us to think about it; Pope emeritus Benedict XVI (as seen above) challenged us to meditate on it; and Pope Francis challenged us to act upon it.

---

[15] Which is why, among others, Collins warns that "today's theology has not yet got the current diaconia right"(pg. 20) and Muller notes that "since the Second Vatican Council and to this day there has been discussion about the exact, specific form of diaconal ministry" (pg. 225). This leads us to the caution given by Echlin, in that "while the services of tomorrow's deacon will be continuous with the ministry of past deacons, it will also be *radically different* (emphasis added) …and that [his] role will be discerned and delineated as it develops in response to tomorrow's needs" (pg. 127-128).

Yet despite fifty years of diaconal presence, confusion and disagreement as to the diaconate being a "true" vocation persists. Why? From my experiences as a teacher, I have found that explaining the simplest of concepts often ends up being the most complex of exercises. Looked at from another perspective, one can find that to travel a short distance can end up being the longest journey one may ever experience (e.g., from one's head, where the knowledge of faith is received, to one's heart, where that faith is accepted). Take this as a case in point: Take the simple letter "a," the first letter of the alphabet. A letter in which some ways can be elemental, yet in others, profound,[16] thus, causing, in certain circumstances the greatest of confusion. For example, putting an "a" before "theism" creates an insurmountable abyss between faith (for now, let it be simply a belief in a reality more than tangible, observable, or measurable) and fatalism (or more commonly becoming known as secularism) where the *only* reality is that which is tangible, observable, and measurable. Here is where the simple letter "a" comes into play; here is where the letter "a" creates confusion; here is where the letter "a" can become fatal, particularly in terms of the dissonance surrounding the question of the diaconate being a "true" vocation. For it can create a

---

[16] The Spiritual Means of the Hebrew Alphabet Letters. WalkingKabbalah.com

perception that a deacon, in the person of a man who being called to, ordained as, and committed to living his call as one of service and not sacrifice, is not living a vocation (in the sense of the man called to the priesthood), but at best an **"a" vocation**.

This is a confusion that persists despite the fact that at the Last Supper, the Lord took the initiative by washing the feet of His disciples to *institute the diaconate*. Why? He did this to show not only His disciples, but all the world, what His Father's will was for those called to the Supper of the Lamb: that they experience His concern and care for them always through the actions of *diakonia*. And this diakonia as Our Lord taught us not only at the Last Supper, but throughout His public ministry, is most effectively carried out in the workplaces, the communities, the homes, and the marketplaces where people live their normal lives.

This is where deacons, not priests, normally live—the secular community, where side by side, step by step, they have their homes, raise their families, and earn their keep (as did Saint Paul). And it is my contention that in constraining one's evaluation of the deacon's activities to that secular pursuit, many (clergy and lay alike) can be led (wrongly) to limiting the deacon's focus as being not vocational but career focused. This is a perception confusing the concept of vocation with career (as discussed above). This is a challenge that despite the *de jure* recognition of the diaconate as a ***true vocation***, the ***de facto*** implications, both official and unofficial, explicit and implicit remain, which is why Kleiber and Lemire, can say, at least in the United States, "***what a deacon is, has yet to be defined***" (emphasis added).[17] This is a challenge that could also apply to the Church in terms of its relationship to—or more specifically its purpose in—the world.

---

[17] *Deacons: Permanent or Passing, An Update on the Permanent of the Catholic Church in the United States*, Richelieu Court Aspen Heights, Slingerlands, NY, pg. 11.

Chapter 3

Sacramental Diakonia:
Essential or Extraneous

When discussing the Order of Deacon, whatever the context, one finds there is a significant consensus among both the clergy and laity regarding what the term diakonia refers to and how it defines the ordained deacon. From that perspective, the challenge is to come to an understanding of *what* that word means, particularly as it relates to *defining* who the deacon is.[18] Thus, this has caused the continuing debate as to whether the Order of Deacon is essential or extraneous to the need for the Church to carry out its mandate given to it by Our Lord at the Last Supper: to serve others as He served them. There is a dissonance manifested in the diverse decisions by a bishop (which I accept is his prerogative) as to whether or not to allow

---

[18] For a fuller discussion on this point, see Collins, *Diakonia*, pg. 45.

deacons to minister to his diocesan flock.

Now, I want to be clear in the use of the terms essential and extraneous. In terms of the Sacrament of Holy Orders, we find His mandate to His apostles—and through them to their successors, the bishops—to be twofold. The mandate *both* offer to His people until He came again the sacrifice He willingly offered on the cross *and* provide those same people His total service to them. But more importantly, these mandates were to be performed in a sacramental (i.e., grace filled) way. This is the reason He empowered them to ordain others with the power to do so, some through their ordination to the priesthood and others through their ordination to the diaconate. That being so, then the Order of Deacon is essential to the carrying out of that mandate.[19] However, if it merely entails providing to others the fruits of the corporal and spiritual works of mercy, then those works can (and, because of

---

[19] A position supported, for example, by Barnett, who states that "[the deacon] above all epitomizes within his…. office the ministry Christ has given to his Church, the servant ministry to which [all are] called and commissioned in [their] baptism" (pg. 141). Echlin supports this when he points out that the deacon "in a special way…is Christ the servant washing the wounded feet of mankind", and does so by bridging "sacred worship and secular worship, horizontal prayer and vertical prayer, the bread of the Eucharist and the bread of pastoral charity" (pg. 129).

one's baptism, should) be rendered to others by all Christians. From such a perspective, the Order of Deacon, while divinely instituted, having an apostolic origin, and being important to carrying out the Lord's mandate in a pastoral, *not* sacramental way, *could* be considered to be extraneous. The determination then of whether the order is essential or not, again, goes back to the meaning of *diakonia*. This is not merely in terms of its secular, or historic meaning, but in the sense that Christ, by His Incarnation, made manifest by both words, when He proclaimed, He came not to be served, but to serve, and by deed at the Last Supper. Christ, in washing the feet of His disciples, mandated they too, must also do.

Thus, the key question, I believe the council raised by the restoration of the Order of Deacon as a permanent presence in the Church's hierarchy is as follows: Is the diaconate an essential or augmentative part of the Church conceived by the Lord on the cross and born at Pentecost a *servant Church?*[20] This leads us to go further and ask ourselves the following: If the Church, Christ's body, is truly a servant Church, as evidenced by the Lord's proclamation that He came to serve and by His washing of His disciples' feet, *which order*, bishop,

---

[20] Causing, as Collins notes, "theological uncertainties and tensions [which are] hampering he development of a theology of the diaconate with which churches and deacons can feel at ease" (pg. 119).

priest or deacon, in terms of their vocational focus, best supports that mandate? Is it the bishop, the successor to the apostles to whom that mandate was first given? Is it the priest, to whom the power was given at his ordination to perpetuate His perfect sacrifice? Or is it the deacon, who by his ordination and by the *normal way* he exercises their particular vocation demonstrates, a servant Church? This Church serves Christ in two ways: in heavenly terms, which equates to the actions of Christ in and through the sacraments, and in worldly terms, which equates to the social dimensions of service, as might clearly be evidenced in the sacramentally strengthened works of mercy, to which the deacon's public ministry is primarily oriented.

Yet despite the Lord's twofold mandate, there is still confusion as to who a deacon is. For although the consensus is that the term deacon implies *service, a* quick review of the literature will show there to be a continuum of understanding as to what that term means. This is a continuum ranging from something as simple as a "waiter," "servant," "social worker," or "helper" to something more significant, such as a "messenger," "envoy", "emissary," "mediating agent," or "representative."

In other words, although the consensus is that the deacon is ordained to serve and that this service is *always* rendered in an intermediary capacity, there is no clear consensus as to what the essential, let alone even general meaning, of the term involves. Thus, before we can determine not only what makes sacramental service distinct, but whether it is necessary and what determines the effectiveness of that service, we need to clarify who it is that the deacon "serves" and more importantly, for whom he is rendering that "service."

Therefore, one must begin at its source—the deacon's ordination by his bishop—to understand, assess the meaning of, and recognize the effectiveness of diaconal efforts. This ordination has a primary function of supporting the bishop in undertaking the mandate he received at his episcopal ordination as a successor to the apostles. This is the same mandate set forth by Jesus at the Last Supper: to not only perpetuate the perfect sacrifice, but also to continue to serve His flock as perfectly demonstrated to His disciples in His washing of their feet. This is a mandate to *both* offer sacrifice and serve. This is a mandate He told them be done ***in persona Christi***, until He comes again in His glory.

Thus, the bishop, as a successor to the apostles, is empowered at his ordination to the episcopate with both the spiritual/sacramental and pastoral needs of the flock in whose care is entrusted to him. In following the example of his predecessors, the apostles, he can be effective in carrying out his mandate. The bishop can empower his priests, through their ordination, with the graces that will enable them to cooperate with him in his spiritual/sacramental ministry. This happens principally by confecting the sacraments as most clearly evidenced by their faculties to offer the Sacrifice of the Mass and the absolution of sin. In a similar sense, the bishop is also able to empower those men he ordains to the Order of Deacon to serve him, through their ordination, with the graces that will enable those deacons to cooperate with him in his pastoral ministry, particularly in their efforts to provide for his flock's needs through their charitable works of mercy. Thus, the completeness of the bishop's efforts in undertaking the spiritual/sacramental and pastoral mandate given to him at his episcopal ordination can only be truly affected through the cooperation and efforts of his priests *and* deacons in their commitment to exercise the distinct mandates given to them at ordination.

These commitments and efforts can be evaluated in terms of their effectiveness. This evaluation must be based on the source of all ministry—whether sacrificial or diaconal in nature: Jesus, the true priest, the true deacon. Taking as our starting point His perfect sacrifice and perfect servanthood, we can see it involves two actions: obedience and humility. The obedience is promised at one's ordination, whether to the priesthood or the diaconate, as Jesus so perfectly demonstrated in the garden of Gethsemane. This is an obedience by which He demonstrated to His apostles then and His disciples now, showing how His genuineness is enhanced, encouraged, and thus effective by a willing offering. That is, it is not coercive, nor merely compliant, but collaborative, an approach that can only lead to cohesiveness. This is an obedience that although always respectful, is not always reactive in essence. This is an obedience that if properly demonstrated, as did Jesus to His Father throughout His public ministry, will always make present the message and love of the one to whom the deacon is obedient. This is an obedience that must always be rendered in a way that brings glory (in whatever form it may take) to the Father.

Significantly, we learn from the Lord, as demonstrated throughout His public ministry, that service must always be offered in humility. This is a humility shown in His relations to those He encountered, whether it was toward those who believed in Him or betrayed Him, those who became His disciples or His detractors, or even those who crucified Him. This is a humility that did not manifest weakness, in whatever form that may appear, but one that evidenced genuine meekness. I learned this lesson well from my experiences at both the Naval Academy and in the Marine Corps. I learned from both example and experience that true meekness is not based on, nor does it entail, weakness. Humility requires an inner strength that is both strong enough and confident enough that one doesn't always have to be "first" or "best" in their relations with others. Thus, it is only in and through these relations with others —particularly in the case of the deacon— whether with the bishop who ordained him, the priests with whom he cooperates, or with the laity he serves, that the true effectiveness of the deacon's "diakonia" can be assessed. These relationships, however, can and often do create challenges to the true understanding of diaconal effectiveness, in terms of the reason for and the focus of that diakonia.

We must start with the fact that it is the bishop alone who places his hands on the deacon at his ordination. This is an action that emphasizes the deacon is first and foremost ordained to serve the bishop in a manner that best enhances the bishop's particular mandate to serve the pastoral needs of his flock. This is a mandate that to be truly effective requires—as Pope Francis often points out— "the smell of the sheep." The bishop must be able to experience where the "sheep" live, work, and play: whether in their neighborhood, in their workplace, or in their marketplace. These are the places where the bishop (and his priests) are not normally found. These are the places where their diakonia, as envisioned by Jesus; by the council; and Pope Francis had the greatest potential to bear fruit. Yet what we commonly find, at least in the United States, is that the usual way deacons are found is relating to the bishop, particularly as evidenced in their assisting him in his pastoral mandate, whether by necessity (e.g., the complexity of the diocesan organization chart) or custom (as referred to earlier, in the sense of the traditional focus on the deacon being a final "step" in the journey to the priesthood). This is a custom that seems to encourage the belief that for a deacon to function effectively in the performance of his diaconal ministry, he needs the close mentorship of a priest. In either instance, the deacon is not truly acting as the bishop's "eyes" and "ears. "This is a situation that tends to hinder the bishop's true appreciation of that "sheep smell. It also minimizes the deacon's "secular experiences" as a resource available to assist the bishop in carrying out his pastoral mandate. Rather, the deacon normally finds himself assigned to a pastor as an additional resource, with the primary focus of augmenting, rather than complementing, the pastor in his parish activities. In short, the result of this makes the assessing of the deacon's diaconal activities effectiveness more complex (if not confusing). It gives credence to the question: Why deacons? After all (with dispensations), a lay person can do all that a deacon does. Such a perception leads directly to assessing not only the viability (usefulness), but the necessity of restoring the diaconate as a permanent order. This is a perception which sees the diaconate as merely a transitory step to the priesthood, the permanent way of sacramentally serving Jesus. This is a perception that requires a response.

When one looks into why that perception is held, one finds that the answer, although profound, is really simple. One must focus on an understanding of not what a deacon does but "who" the deacon is. Therefore, it must be approached from a Christological perspective. In taking that approach, we find the question that really needs to be asked: Does or does not the deacon better enable the bishop to carry out his mandate to better serve Christ in others? This is a perspective from which the answer becomes clear. Over the long haul, serving Christ in others cannot be as successful without the graces conferred on the ordained deacon as it can be with those diaconal graces.

It is my contention that it is from this Christological baseline—the actions of Jesus at the Last Supper—that we cannot only say yes in confirming the wisdom of the bishops at the council, as well of that of Pope Saint Paul VI, that the restoration of the Order of Deacon to its proper and "***permanent*** place in the Church, was proper but also essential."[21] This perspective gives us the means for truly assessing the effectiveness of the deacon's sacramental diakonia.

---

[21] Catechism of the Catholic Church Articles 1536,1537

For it is the application of his particular charisms, whether sacramental or personal, in his serving Christ in those persons that the answer lies. Because it is not only those he encounters in the Church, but those he encounters in the marketplace where he purchases the necessities of life, the workplace where he earns his livelihood, or the community in which he lives, that his diaconal effectiveness must be deterined.

This an important and essential discriminator in assessing diaconal effectiveness. To paraphrase Pope Francis, one can say that diakonia begins in the sheepfold, whether that sheepfold be the home, the community, the workplace, or the parish where His sheep are to be found in the presence of the Good Shepherd, both sacramentally and pastorally. In his vision, I see him establishing a diaconal model for a diakonia that must not only be exercised, but also culminate in and among the "sheep *"where they are found.* This, then, is where the effectiveness of the ordained diaconate is to be determined.

Jesus mandated His apostles to continue this form of service in His name, each in the particular and sacramental way he was called. So, through ordination, they are challenged to go out into the world (each in the manner appropriate to their degree of ordination) and not only tell by their words, but show by their actions, what Jesus intended the diakonia to be.

So now we can look at measuring the effectiveness of

diakonia. This effectiveness can only be measured by the Lord's actions throughout His public ministry. These actions and words, by which He shows us that diaconal efforts/activities, of whatever nature, can only be effective in and through relationships. These are not merely relationships that arise through ritualistic practices, such as participating in the liturgy or in the confecting of sacraments, but pastorally, in and through the deacon's "extra liturgical" activities so to speak, where his relationships with others are bound up with the various works of mercy, whether with his bishop, not only in the deacon's assistance to him in serving his flock, but in informing him as to what, from their living in the same "sheepfold," the deacon has found the flock to need. These are actions he needs to share with his pastor and his brother priests, with whom he finds himself cooperating with at the parish level. He must bring to them, the "smell" of the sheep, whether parishioners or not. Most importantly, however, in terms of effective diakonia, it is the people with whom the deacon lives, works, and interacts with in the normal course of both his sacramental and secular activities that will determine its effectiveness.

This is the arena in which the deacon's effectiveness is assessed. The place where the deacon finds his diaconal activities to be effective is shown by how he enables those he interacts with to see Christ's presence and actions in his diaconal actions, but more importantly, in interacting with them, enabling him to recognize Christ in those same people he was ordained to serve. These people may be, for example, like the prodigal son, the good thief on the cross, the disciple who doubted him, or even the one who betrayed him. These are His brothers and sisters, images of His Father, in whom the Holy Spirit either dwells or desires to be one with.

Relationships must be reassessed from all perspectives to understand the effectiveness of sacramental diakonia: sacramental, ecclesiastical, pastoral, and personal. For it is my contention that for the deacon's role to be recognized as at least a critical aspect of the Church's efforts to be successful, it must be assessed in terms of the mandate Christ gave His apostles. Christ demonstrated that this mandate cannot be done merely within the "confines" of the "official" Church boundaries (however defined). It must also take into account the "unofficial" environment, the secular world, in which the deacon lives his vocation and where neither the priest nor bishop are normally found.

Using the analogy of the "telephone" game will help make this point. A message is created by the first person and is passed along to the other players until it is returned to the originator. The resulting message barely, if at all, resembles the original message. In fact, studies show that even in the best of organizations, the distortion of a message increases with the number of intermediaries involved between the sender and the receiver.[22] And, thus, in terms of the present scheme of things within the Church's hierarchy, we find both the bishop, who in carrying out his plan for serving his flock and those members of his flock who desire to make their bishop aware of their needs or concerns, find themselves playing "telephone."

---

[22] Downward communication is when a message starts at the higher echelons of a traditional organizational hierarchy and is passed down, level by level, to the lower ranks who will actually implement the action. The problem with this type of message transmission is that information will usually be lost as it goes down from one level to another. One study found that downward communication over the course of five organizational levels lost about 80% of the information by the time it cleared the fifth level. Quizlet.com/Chapter 11 Communication and Information Technology

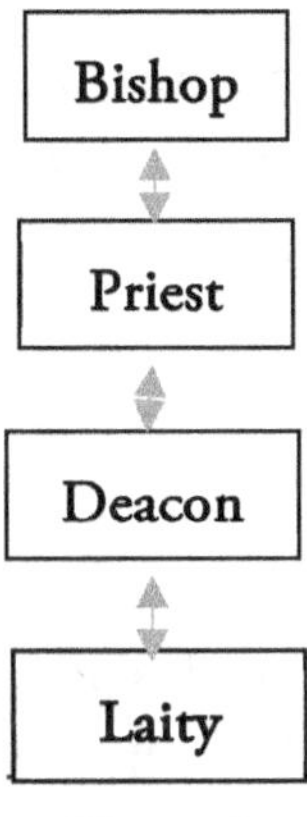

Figure 1

As shown in Figure 1, the bishop who originates a message, in whatever form, customarily passes it along to his flock through his priests, who then (albeit not always) pass it along to his deacons, who, by virtue of their situation, are asked to pass that message on to the laity. Looking at it from the bottom up, one can easily see a similar pattern emerging from the laity to the bishop. In refocusing on the relationship (at least from the sacramental laying on of hands) of the bishop and the deacon, a more effective means of the deacon serving not only the bishop, but his flock, is proposed in Figure 2. Here, we find the bishop, along with his priests **and** deacons, are in direct relationships with his flock. But that relationship goes a step further. This allows relationships, particularly as they relate to bishop–deacon relationships, to be restored to the original intent for which the Order of Deacon was instituted by Christ at the Last Supper. This is an order first brought to fruition by the apostles in ordaining Stephen and his six brothers[23] to assist them in serving those entrusted to them by the same Christ. And it is a relationship, unfortunately, that can usually only be found ceremonially. Yet it is a relationship that if restored, will provide the bishop (and, by extension, his priests) with less distortion of both the bishop's message to his flock and their message to him.

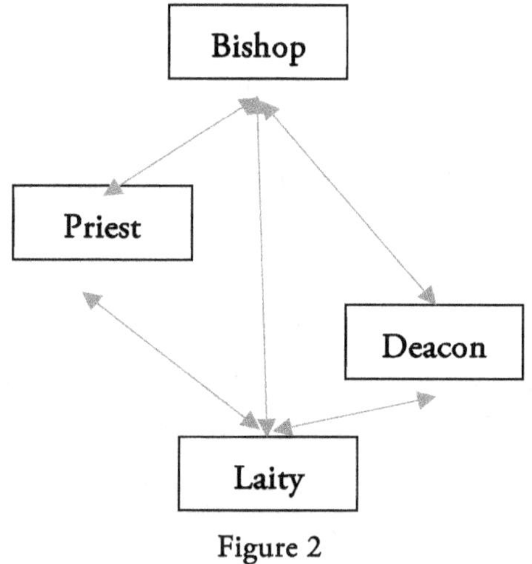

Figure 2

---

[23] Philip, Prochorus, Nicanor, Timon, Parmmenas, and Nicolaus (Acts 6:5)

This is a relationship that will contribute to greater effectiveness, not only in the "intra" Church but "extra" Church. This will bring the "smells" (needs) of the laity to the bishop and his priests, while simultaneously bringing to the laity an example of how to live their particular form of diakonia through the mandate given to them by their baptism. In short, one can say that the effectiveness of the sacramental diakonia can only be assessed by how the ordained deacon exercises that vocation in both the Church and the community in which he lives, works, and plays. This is not in the way that *all* the baptized are called to diakonia but in the particular way that his sacramental diakonia makes Christ's presence not only known, but experienced, by those he serves.

Thus, for a deacon to be effective in terms of his diaconal ministry, that ministry, in collaboration with, yet distinct from the priest, must in some way clearly imitate Jesus, the perfect servant. These diaconal efforts must be focused on serving all people, in every situation they are found, particularly those who are not found in the mainstream. Looking at Christ's public ministry, we find it is a diakonia that must have one focus, one purpose, and one end: to reveal to those served the depths of God's love for them as well as, the extent to which He would go for them to experience that love. This is the standard by which the deacon's diaconal service must be measured and identified.

Chapter 4
Bishop-Priest-Deacon Relationships

It has been fifty years since the Order of Deacon was restored to its proper and permanent place in the hierarchy of Holy Orders. Yet there continues to remain a general sense of confusion as to the relationship of this restored order to that of the presbyterate and the episcopate in a more general sense. Because from whatever perspective you look at it, the reality is that the diaconate is here to stay. The result is that these relationships will be a necessity and continue to exist. So how do we go about moving forward? I believe it can be done by recognizing that there are four ways to describe bishop-priest-deacon relationships: sacramentally, fraternally, functionally, and pastorally. More importantly, it must be understood, that if true progress is to be made, then we must look at these ways as being neither independent nor competitive with each other but instead linked in a distinct and definite way.

Sacramentally

Now any effort to truly get a handle on these relationships must start from a sacramental perspective.[24] One must begin with the origins of the Sacrament of Holy Orders. There is no debate that the Sacrament of Holy Orders was instituted by Jesus at the Last Supper. What is open to discussion for some, however, is what it was that Jesus instituted. From the events described in the synoptic Gospels, there is no question that the Lord, to perpetuate His impending sacrifice on the cross, commanding His apostles to do what He just did, instituted the priesthood. But I believe that if we stop there, we do not get the full picture or intent of Jesus in His deliberate and determined decision to institute the Sacrament of Holy Orders. More importantly, we do not grasp His intention for doing so. To achieve that objective, I propose, we must also look to the description of the Last Supper given to us by Saint John in the thirteenth chapter of his Gospel. There we find the actions of Our Lord which are not found in the synoptic Gospels:

So, during supper, fully aware that the Father had put everything into his power and that he had come from God and was returning to God, he rose from supper and took off his outer garments. He took a towel and tied it around his waist. He came

---

[24] Gerhard Muller, *Priesthood and Diaconate*, pg. 142

to Simon Peter, who said to him "Master, are you going to wash my feet?" Jesus answered and said to him, "What I am doing, you do not understand now, but you will understand later." So, when he had washed their feet [and] put his garments back on and reclined at table again, he said to them, "Do you realize what I have done for you? You call me 'teacher' and 'master,' and rightly so, for indeed I am. If I, therefore, the master and teacher, have washed your feet, you ought to wash one another's feet. I have given you a model to follow, so that as I have done for you, you should also do" (Jn. 13: 2, 7, 12, and 15) [emphasis added].

What we find here is Jesus going beyond His mandate to His apostles that they become priests and thus act in the person of Christ, the head. In return, they are able to offer the Holy Sacrifice of the Mass to the world in His stead. He goes on to command that they also become deacons and act in the person of Christ, the servant. In return, they are able to serve the world also in His stead.

From what we are told in the Catechism of the Catholic Church (hereafter referred to as CCC),the apostles and their successors, the bishops in union with the pope, possess the "fullness of the Sacrament of Holy Orders[25]"—a truth manifested in the narrations of the Last Supper as set forth in

---

[25] Catechism of the Catholic Church (CCC), Article 1536

the gestalt *of all four Gospels*. In short, this is the fullness of *both the priesthood and the diaconate*. This is why it can only be the bishop, as a successor to the apostles, who can "pass on" the faculties granted to him by the Lord at the Last Supper. The bishop can bestow this both to those men who are called to perpetuate that sacrifice and to those men who are called to be of perpetual service to him.

We find then in the Lord's institution of the Sacrament of Holy Orders and the mandate He gave His apostles and through them their successors, the bishops, the origin of their faculty to ordain both priests and deacons. This is a mandate as we learn in Acts that their successors continued to do so, as well. Thus, we can see that the faculties of the priest emanate from that mandate that continues in the person of the bishop. In that same sense, the faculties of the deacon emanate from that same source —the bishop. Because of this dependency on the bishop, the relationship between the priest and a deacon can be said to be determined largely by the culture and customs observed through the behavior the bishop. This refers not only to the actions he exercises with his priests, but more significantly, that which he exercises with his deacons. This is a relationship that hasn't been experienced in the Latin Church for over a millennium.

In other words, the relationship between the priest and the

deacon can only be fruitful through their interrelationship with the bishop. This is a fact that makes it apparent that their ministries, their vocations, and their particular calls are not separate but interrelated. They are not *different,* in the sense of a "distance" between the two vocations, but *distinct.* This is a distinction identified by the Lord at the Last Supper when He instituted at the same event both the priesthood and the diaconate. And it is made manifest at every Mass of the Lord's Supper on Holy Thursday, where the bishop, who holds the fullness of the sacrament, and the priest, his coworker ordained to sacrifice, perform the diaconal function of washing the feet of the Lord's disciples. This is evidenced by Pope Francis, who, in performing that action, was seen to wear his stole as a deacon, not as a priest.

These are actions that, particularly regarding the Sacrament of Holy Orders, bring to light the Lord's mandate to His apostles at the Last Supper, one that in the synoptic Gospels emphasize the Lord's focus on the institution of the priesthood for the express purpose of giving to those men He chose to do so the faculties to continue to offer His one, perfect sacrifice. Whereas in John, for some *specific and inspired reason,* His mandate to His apostles and their successors, to call other men to *the diaconate* for continuing to serve others as He served them is emphasized. These are specific actions on His part from which we find the seeds that would grow into the threefold Sacrament of Holy Orders. However, the deacon is *not*, by his specific call, equated to the priest in terms of the hierarchy *nor* in function. Rather, we find in the sacramental mandate given by Our Lord, that *all*—whether called to be bishops, priests, or deacons—are called through the distinction of their particular form of sacramental discipleship to *service, each in his distinct way*. This is one reason why I believe the Order of Deacon is conferred on *all the ordained*, whether their call is to the episcopate, the priesthood, or the diaconate.

This is a distinction clearly described in Saint John's Gospel. For in looking at the passage, we can see that once the supper was over (i.e., once the Mass, at which the priest has the mandate to preside, was over), He rose and "took off his garments" (as does the deacon when the mass is over, and takes off his liturgical "garments"). Then, we find Him going to Peter (as does the deacon go to those who had attended the mass, whether they be found in the neighborhood in which the deacon lives or the workplace where the deacon earns his living) and served him, in washing his feet, serving him in the humblest of ways (as does the deacon most commonly away from the "spotlight" of the parish). When He was done, we find Him putting back on His garments and returning to the table *as a deacon does*, when, returning from living in the neighborhood or at work, comes back to the altar, puts on his liturgical vestments, and shares with his bishop or those priests he is assigned to serve. These are experiences evidenced, at least symbolically, through his reading aloud the Prayers of the Faithful at the Mass at which he serves.

The actions by the Lord at the Last Supper give evidence that there was both recognition and acceptance of the distinct orders of the sacrament from the beginning. Saint Paul's description of the expectations for both a bishop (priest) and a deacon as well as are set forth in the pastoral letters of some of the early Church Fathers such as Origen and Anastasius. The question is why now, some 2000 years later, is there still confusion as to that relationship?

Fraternally

In attempting to understand the fraternal relationship between a bishop, his priests, and his deacons, as well as those between deacons and priests, let me reflect on my family relationships growing up We were an Italian family growing up in a close-knit Bronx community. Besides my father and brother, I had seven uncles and sixty-eight first cousins. Looking back on the dynamics that I experienced within my family, I found a model by which I believe best describe the relationship of the dynamics that exist between the three grades of Holy Orders.

In looking at the relationships that I experienced with my father, brother, uncles, and cousins, I came to see the bishop in terms of his relationship with his priests and deacons. This is a relationship that finds the bishop taking the role of a father to his priests (in effect, his sons) and that of an uncle to his deacons (in effect, his nephews). What is most important to take away from this analogy, however, is that they are *all from the same family* and, thus, in terms of the relationships between priests and deacons, that of one between cousins.

Now, why is that significant in terms of *understanding* that relationship? Again, going back to my family experiences, there were some uncles with whom I had a closer relationship than they did with their sons; and some of my cousins got along better with my father than I did. There were also some cousins I was more comfortable with compared to my own brother (and cousins my brother was more comfortable with than he was with me). There were other cousins, while still my cousins, that I did not have the same closeness. Yet when something relating to one's immediate family as opposed to the family as a whole (which I found to happen but very rarely), without exception, the son always took precedence over the nephew, and the brother always took precedence over the cousin.

Thus, in terms of bishop-priest-deacon relationships, there will be occasions when the bishop might be more (or less) comfortable in terms of his relationship with a deacon than with a priest, but the deacon will always recognize that, when using the above analogy, he is a nephew and not, like a priest, a son. Likewise, in terms of priest–deacon relationships, while recognizing a cousin-like relationship exists, neither loses sight of who, in terms of the bishop, is the son and who is the nephew.

This is a dynamic then that has more to do with relationship (i.e., family) than personality (i.e., organizationally). This has to do more with paternalism than preference. In short, it is a relationship that is not in itself effective or ineffective but realistic. Realizing this fact, we find the dynamics between the three, at whatever level, focusing on one of two things: on sibling/parental relationships, which can lead to dysfunctionality, or on the familial relationship, thus enabling a more synergistic and more productive form of ministry to exist. This is a ministry that would be consistent with the mandate given at the ordination to each grade. How? This is done by the emphasis of the family elder, parent/uncle, in the person of the bishop, to not only encourage between his priests and deacons, but practice in relationship with them, fraternal harmony. This is one way (again from family experiences) to hold both intimate family gatherings (as parents do with their siblings) and larger family reunions (as uncles and aunts do with their children and nephews) As I have learned from my family experiences, the more familiar or comfortable one was with their siblings or cousins and they with their parents and uncles, the more genuine, the more loving, and (some fifty plus years later), the more synergistic that relationship would be.

Why do I believe that? Because although one can come to like or dislike another a person whom they don't know personally, they cannot love that person. This is a truth anyone who has loved can attest to. Although one can be attracted to or put off by a person they don't know personally, they cannot love that person. This is a reality upon that sums up the Lord's mandate to all His disciples. What better way to look at their commitment to living His mandate than within the family bishop, priests, and deacons are members of?

Functionally

Whether ordained to teach, to offer sacrifice, or to serve, all grades of Holy Orders have one mandate—the mandate given by the Lord immediately prior to His return to His Father: "Go out into the whole world" and "teach [each and every person your ministry brings you into contact with] to observe everything I commanded you."[26] This is a mandate that carries

---

[26] Matthew 28:19-20

a simple, yet profound message: repent, believe the Good News. This is a mandate to let all know that God is a merciful God, that God is a forgiving God, but, most importantly, that God is a loving God, who so loves us He became man to demonstrate that love by dying for us.

Now, not until one comes to realize just what that message entails, will anyone possessing any of the sacramental grades of Holy Orders find it hard to recognize the only effective means by which to do so. Only by emulating the actions of the One whose gave us that mandate. The One who lived His earthly ministry truly practicing it. The One who commanded those who said yes to His call to Holy Orders to live that call in a uniquely, sacramentally way which was "to love one another as He loves them"(Jn. 13:34). And to do so, as the deacon Saint Francis of Assisi reminded his friend Brother Leo, "not by words, but by actions." Yet these are not any actions, mind you, but actions that entail nothing less than direct and personal relationships, regardless of what particular form their ministry entails.

Thinking of this challenge brings to mind an experience I had some fifty years ago when sitting in the field house at the United States Naval Academy, waiting to be commissioned a second lieutenant in the Marine Corps. The then Commandant of the Marine Corps, after swearing me and fifty-eight of my classmates in, looked at us standing there. He was wearing four stars and the Medal of Honor, among other numerous trappings of office, and we were wearing nothing but bare uniforms. He said to us: "Gentlemen, I envy you! "This is a message I could not accept as true until some years later in turning over my platoon of marines to my successor, to become, within a year the company commander. This is an action by which I learned that I was, and would not again be, in a direct, interpersonal relationship with these marines. The further I advanced in rank, the more distant that direct relationship became. No matter how often I spent time with my marines, whether in peacetime or combat, there was always someone, in terms of having a direct interpersonal relationship, between me and them. And then, I came to understand what the commandant was saying to me that day in June. Because I also envied that second lieutenant who had a direct interpersonal relationship with his marines.

These are experiences by which I was better able to understand the relationships between the deacon, who through his normal mandate to live his vocation in the world, whether as a cook, baker, candlestick maker, teacher, clerk, banker, or engineer, can have a direct, personal relationship with others, that neither the priest nor bishop can have, however dedicated they may be to knowing their parishioners.

This is a reality that better helped me to understand the relationship that ought to exist between the bishop (and/or his priest representatives) and the deacon. For, although it is in the bishop's mandate to care for all the souls in his diocese, he cannot really get their pulse, their concerns, their spiritual needs in the way a deacon can because of where he normally lives his vocation. This is a fact the Church recognizes, albeit symbolically: it is the deacon, who through the Prayers of the Faithful, is the one to normally present to the church the worldly and spiritual needs of the people, because it is their community, he lives his vocation.

This is a reality that Pope Francis recognizes by his constant challenge to his priests to go out into the neighborhoods where the people live, to feel their pulse, their pain, and their concerns; this is asking them to do what his deacons are doing. This is a fact articulated to me in a different but powerful way in a conversation I had with a priest in the parish we were both assigned when he said, "Nick, the difference between you [a deacon] and me [a priest] is that 95% of the people I see are, in one way or another, in need of, and thus seeking Christ, while 95% of the people you see who are also in need of Christ but are not normally seeking Him."[27] Or as a brother deacon noted with a different slant: from a pastoral perspective that people come to the priest for Christ's graces, whereas people come to the deacon for Christ's comfort.

And, in returning to Our Lord's mandate, this mandate could better be undertaken; more effective, and thus more productive, if the deacon, mandated by his order to live among those who Pope Francis identifies as "sheep," is encouraged by those he serves (his bishop and his priests) to pay attention to their "smell" (to use the pope's word).

The question then is why is that not happening, at least not consistently enough? Before answering that question, however, one needs to go back to the Last Supper and recognize that bishops, through their relationship to the apostles, possess *the fullness of the sacrament,* by which they are challenged to continue carrying out the mandate given to them by the Lord. This is a mandate to perpetuate His sacrifice, by ordaining men to the presbyterate, by which they will become his coworkers

---

[27] In discussing this point with a brother deacon, he gave me a different slant on what the priest was trying to say: from his experience, he felt that one might say from a pastoral perspective that people come to the priest for Christ's graces, whereas people come to the deacon for Christ's comfort. To me, from a general perspective, it was an interesting concept.

yet without possessing the same fullness of orders. This is evidenced by the fact that as priests, they do not share in the bishop's *successorship*. Thus, if the priest, the bishop's designated coworker, is not in possession of the fullness of the sacrament, what does that say about the deacon? The deacon was also determined in a similar way for the apostles and their successors, to perpetuate His mandate to serve Him in others. Because the deacon, like the priest, also does not possess the charism of succession. But neither does he possess the charism of sacrifice, which a priest does. Clearly, then, the man ordained to the Order of Deacon is ordained "not to sacrifice, but to service."[28]

In continuing with the family analogy as a means for understanding the relationship between a priest and a deacon, let us now look at the role that exists between cousins. By doing so, I contend that although the relationship between a deacon and a priest can be looked at as familial, it is not" intimate." Thus, their relationships and interactions entail a different range of dynamics than what is found between brother priests.

---

[28] Yet as Echlin points out, although then deacon's "charism is different," he is not "lower than" nor "inferior to" the priest in terms of seeing Christ's total mandate given to His apostles, and now, the responsibility of their successors is carried out effectively. See the reflections below on the concept of synergy.

These relationships and dynamics, however, need not nor should affect the exercising of their distinct vocations in a synergistic manner, whether individually or collaboratively.

Yet the relationship does create dynamics that can and do lead to a more complex set of interactions. These are interactions that can bring about an environment in which these interactions tend to be more routinely exercised, rather than pastorally effective.

The potential for this confusion can be found to originate in the experiences of a man who functioned as a deacon, in transition to his ordination to the priesthood. As a priest, in looking at the deacon who serves with him perceives from his own experiences, someone who needed direction as to what his functions entailed. And by taking that perspective, may (and often does) lose out on the opportunity to avail himself of the experiences the deacon brings to the table. In short, one may say the priest in doing so, shunts the all too many available "cooks", "bakers" and "candlestick makers "to the sidelines.

Returning to the analogy of the father/uncle (bishop) and his "sons" (priests) and nephews (deacons), one can see a major reason why this is so. For priests, much like brothers, know from their familial intimacy the strengths and weaknesses of their brother priests and can be there to use their brothers' strengths to enhance the parish/diocese efforts in doing the

Lord's work and to encourage and support them in their weaknesses. However, in the relationship between cousins (i.e., priest–deacon relationships), it takes greater effort and willingness to get to know one's cousins, and this involves a willingness on the part of *both* to reach out and share (albeit in different degrees) their strengths and weaknesses so that a truly effective "family" effort can be exercised in doing His will.

This is an effort that not only can be done but is being done effectively in more and more instances. The success of this can be attributed to two factors. The first is the willingness of the priest to look beyond the limited presence of the deacon and what he is in pertaining to his place in the hierarchy. This is an exercise that will expose him to the deacon's experiences and expertise and that can be fruitfully brought to bear in his exercising his ministry. The second rests with the deacon (as it does with cousins), asking deacons to extend themselves in a way that presents to the priest a more complete picture of the deacon as person. This is a task that requires the deacon to do so in a respectful but proactive way. For by sharing with those (from whoever's perspective one takes) who are in fact (albeit extended) family, not only will the fraternal bonds be strengthened, but the functional efforts will be more effective.

Pastorally

The effectiveness of these relationships must be looked at from two perspectives. The first is the distinct ways each are mandated to exercise their particular vocations. The second is the manner in which each particular vocation brings them into contact with both parishioners and non-parishioners. By doing so, one can gain a better understanding of not only the uniqueness of the deacon's ministry, but its complementarity with those of the bishop and priest. This complementarity must be not merely acknowledged, but encouraged both by the bishop and the priest. In doing so, the deacon's efforts will not only support but enhance the bishop and the priest in exercising their distinct ministries.

The deacon, although *like* the priest, is set *apart* from the laity by his ordination, but *unlike* the priest, he is not set *aside* from the laity by his ordination. Why? Because through the sacramental graces received at his ordination, the deacon can, by living his vocation *among* the laity, more effectively energize, empower, and encourage the laity by example. In doing so, he has the unique opportunity of encouraging them to realize that they too can live their baptismal calling in a way that they will make Christ's presence known to the world. This is an experience seen by the laity as they observe the deacon living his vocation shoulder to shoulder with them.

In doing so, the deacon will accomplish two things. First, the deacon will enable the needs, desires, and priorities of the laity to be made known first hand to both his bishop and his priests. Second, he will, by where he lives his vocation, be in a better position to respond to those needs timelier and more effective as well. Therefore, for the Church's response to be realistic, the bishop-priest-deacon relationship must be a synergistic unity of functions/focus/purpose if it is to be an effective vehicle for responding to Christ's mandate to serve Him in others, not only where they worship, but also at where they work and live.

The deacon, therefore, is in a position where he can more realistically integrate the things rendered to Caesar through the particular career and lifestyle challenges his experiences have given him and rendered to God through his threefold ministry of liturgy, word, and charity. From this position, particularly in terms of establishing effective/synergistic relationships between him and the bishop and his priests, the deacon can best be looked at as not only a "go-between" (interestingly enough, one of the accepted translations for the definition of a deacon) but as the union between the laity and the bishop and priest, to whom their spiritual and sacramental care and welfare is primarily entrusted.

Yet, although one recognizes the commonality of the

bishop's, priest's, and deacon's commitment in their efforts to the care of the sheep, one must also recognize the distinction in how they not only exercise their particular vocations in doing so, but also the way in which they are called to do so. A relationship which must be synergistic to be effective.

I will use Figures 3 through 6, to explain these relationships in terms of the three-fold mandate of sacrifice, service and teaching given to Jesus to His apostles, and through them to their successors, the bishops. I will first look at these mandates as I see them as applying to each of the three grades of Holy Orders in Figures 3 to 5 below. Then I will identify in Figure 6 the area of commonality that I believe must be focused on if the relationships between bishops, priests, and deacons are to be truly effective in their carrying out the mandates given them through their ordinations. In illustrating each Order's commitment to the three mandates, I will attempt to show the relative degree of commitment each of the Orders have to each mandate.

In terms of the bishop, it requires us to first recognize the bishop is given both the mandate Our Lord gave his apostles/bishops, to offer to his flock His sacrifice in memory of Him and to serve them as He did. Then before returning to His Father, He mandated they carry out His commission to teach the world all that He had taught and did for them (see Figure 3).

Jesus' commission to teach the world all that He has done and said	
Jesus' mandate to offer His perfect *sacrifice* to the world in memory of Him until He comes again	Jesus' mandate to *serve* others as He has served you and they them

Figure 3. The Bishop's Vocational Commitment

Through this empowerment, the bishop in turn can enable his priests through their ordination to share in a most intimate and ontological way the sacerdotal priesthood (see Figure 2), which the deacon does not. This is a relationship through and by which the Lord's mandate to perpetuate His perfect sacrifice on the cross until He comes again is assured. This mandate is essential to the existence of Jesus' Church, a mandate that is in no way shared with, but again through the empowerment of the bishop, is assisted in by the deacon (see Figure 5).

Jesus' Commission to teach the world all that He has done and said	
Jesus' mandate to offer His perfect *sacrifice* to the world in memory of Him until He comes again	Jesus' mandate to *serve* others as He has served you and you them

Figure 4. The Priest's Vocational Commitment

	Jesus' commission to teach the world all that He has done and said
	Jesus' mandate to *serve* others as He has served you and you them

Figure 5. The Deacon's Vocational Commitment

Yet the Lord's mandate did not stop there. For He went on, after the meal to also mandate through the same sacrament instituted at that Last Supper, His ministry of Sacramental service to others must also continue until He returns. And so, the successors of those apostles to whom He gave those mandates, the bishops, as did the apostles, while ordaining priests to serve as their coworkers in continuing to offer that same sacrifice, they also ordained deacons to assist them in serving those entrusted to them through their ordination to the episcopate.

In a similar albeit essentially distinct way, the bishop, therefore, in undertaking his episcopal vocation, needs not only to have an intimate relationship with his priests, but he must also have a direct relationship with his deacons[29]. This is a relationship that if it is to be truly effective, must be one that is not merely social nor haphazard but regular and focused on the ways in which his deacons can constructively assist him in achieving the mandate: to shepherd the flock entrusted to him. This is a flock that is not normally to be found in and around the Church proper, but in the workplace and community in

---

[29] A more "formal" picture of the relationships between a bishop, his priests, and his deacons can be found in the National Directory. See articles 41–47 for that of the bishop and his priests and articles 48–49 for that of the bishop and his deacons.

which they live their discipleship and where the deacon, in exercising his vocation, is also found.

This is a relationship, however, if it is to be effective, cannot focus on the differences or even the distinctions of the three vocations but must focus on the area of commonality (or union), as illustrated in Figure 6. This is where we find the union of the three not in sacrifice, but in teaching and service. In the case of service, we can find the common efforts of all three orders, both in the distinct ways their vocation leads them (e.g., for the bishop to complete for his flock the sacraments of initiation through the confecting of the Sacrament of Confirmation, the priest to provide the sinner with absolution or healing through the Sacraments of Healing, or the deacon by witnessing and blessing the love of a man and a women entering into the Sacrament of Marriage and the common ways the three provide others, for example, in pastoral visits, social services, or sacramental preparation.

	Jesus' commission to teach the world all that He has done and said	
	Jesus' mandate to *serve* others as He has served you and you them	

Figure 6. The Area of Commonality

Chapter 5

Challenges

In the eyes of the Church, fifty years is but a blink. Yet in the fifty years since the diaconate was restored to its proper and permanent place in the Church's hierarchy, there are still challenges.[30] These are challenges by which the Church, if it accepts them, will enable the diaconate to not only be recognized, but accepted for what it is. More importantly, it

---

[30] This is a reality pointed out, for example, by Kleiber and Lemire, in saying that "what a deacon is, has yet to be clearly established" (pg. 11), or as Plater notes, "attempts to restore the order have caused controversy, debate and *resistance* [emphasis added] in some places" (pg. 2); As Osborne notes, "the reestablishment of the permanent deaconate has engendered some major theological, pastoral, and personal issues of a confrontational nature (pgs. 94-95). I think the point is best summed up by Collins in stating that "...theological uncertainties and tensions of today [regarding the diaconate] are hampering the development of a theology of the diaconate with which churches and *deacons* [emphasis added] can feel at ease."

will enable the Church to reenergize and revitalize the Body of Christ in terms of its servant nature. In doing so, it will enable not only its members, but the world in which it lives, to truly experience the One who came not to be served, but to serve.

With that objective in mind, I offer from my experiences the following challenges those experiences uncovered. Addressing them properly, will more effectively reintegrate married men into the Sacrament of Holy Orders, particularly as it relates to the Order of Deacon. It will enable the Church to not only determine, but to recognize, the reality of the deacon's vocation. This will accomplish several things. It will first refocus the Church's approach to diaconal ordination and assignment. By doing so, it will encourage the restoration of the bishop–deacon relationship to its original objective. Further, it will initiate those efforts necessary to focus on the Sacrament of Holy Orders as being a synergistic relationship rather than a mere organizational one. This is a critical distinction because the Church can trace it roots, in terms of its structure, to the Roman administrative structure that was in place at the time of its birth. Yet the Church, at the same time, found its strength not in its organizational structure, but in its pastoral practices. These are practices where the functioning of the apostles/bishops were effective in their personal missionary efforts to bring Christ, both in Sacrament and Word, to those who had not yet been experienced by Him. The success of this can in large part be related to how those efforts were supported by their deacons.[31]

---

[31] I have deliberately chosen not to address such controversial issues as, for example, that of women ordination to the diaconate (as some both within the church and outside the church are proposing). I have done so because I firmly believe that the magisterium specifically, and Saint John Paul II so eloquently in his encyclical, are at least *implicitly* saying *the same as to the ordination of women to the diaconate*. Why do I say that? Because although it was Jesus in His human *manhood* who offered for us His perfect sacrifice perpetually through the person of the *men* he installed as His first priests to act in the person of that same Christ, the Holy Sacrifice of the Mass, it was also in His human *manhood* that He demonstrated the essence of draconian His washing of His disciples feet, the same diaconia entrusted to those *men* acting in the person of the same Christ (albeit not as Christi capitus, but *Christi servitus*). Nor do I address, from a more pastoral level, the issue of deacons, who tend to find themselves in many instances, while undertaking their vocation of service, spending a great deal of time and effort with the sick and dying in hospitals and nursing homes, having the faculties to administer the Sacrament of Anointing of the Sick (an argument well researched and posited for those interested in that issue by John Ziegler in his book *Let Them Anoint the Sick*, The Liturgical Press, Collegeville, MN).

Challenge 1: The Reintegration of Married Men into Holy Orders

One of the challenges in accepting the restored diaconate to its proper place in the Church's hierarchy is the eligibility for married men to be ordained, albeit, in the Latin Rite, which is limited to the Order of Deacon. This challenge appears at several levels: traditional, ecclesiastical, and practical.

Despite what many think, clerical celibacy has not always been either expected nor the norm for ordination. In fact, other than John, Church historians cannot claim that any of the other original twelve apostles were celibate. In fact, we know from Scripture that Peter, to whom Our Lord gave the command to "feed His sheep" and who the Church from that moment on recognized as the first pope, *was* married. We even hear Saint Paul, who like Our Lord, chose the celibate state, pointing in his letter to Timothy that not only were there married deacons in the apostolic Church, but married bishops as well.

Yet as the Church grew in experience and practice, the merits of celibacy became more recognized as the "better way" of serving the One who came to serve us. Quickly reviewing the Church's journey through time, celibacy, which was for the first millennium an option, gradually became a preferred and then mandatory way of serving Him and His Church in the Sacrament of Holy Orders[32]. This is a practice that remained in effect (at least in the Latin Rite Church) until Saint Pope Paul VI, acting on the initiative of the Council Fathers at VC II, issued his Moto Propotu, by which the Latin Rite Church was reintroduced to a married clergy. A situation that the church finds itself having to reacquaint itself with.

Before we address this challenge, however, it must be noted that we find there seems to be an emphasis on married men when identifying candidates for the newly restored Order of Deacon. This is a perception supported by CARA statistics that identify that over 90% of presently ordained deacons to the restored order are married[33]. This is an implicit bent that posits

---

[32] Although the decrees of the Second Council of the Lateran might still be interpreted in the older sense of prohibiting marriage only after ordination, they came to be understood as absolute prohibitions, and, while the fact of being married was formally made a canonical impediment to ordination in the Latin Church only with the 1917 Code of Canon Law, Canon 987, the prohibition of marriage for all clerics in major orders began to be taken simply for granted. (See John W. O'Malley, *The History behind Celibacy and the Priesthood*, America, The Jesuit Review, October 28, 2002) The Second Lateran Council is thus often cited as having for the first time introduced a general law of celibacy, requiring ordination only of unmarried men.
[33] As of 2018, 92% of deacons in the United States are married. A Portrait of the Permanent Diaconate: A Study for the U.S. Catholic

if an unmarried man feels called to serve Christ in and through the Sacrament of Holy Orders, the "best" way to do so is as a priest. This, despite the reality that the policy of the Church (as pointed out by VCII and Pope Saint Paul VI) is that married men *may not* be the only way to be ordained to the diaconate.

And it is here that the challenge is raised. This is a challenge found in the perception that if a married man is called to the vocation of being one with his wife in living the Sacrament of Marriage, how can he then have a vocation to Holy Orders? This is a challenge made more complex to some in that the Church (rightly so) admonishes the married deacon that *marriage comes first!* This is a point made clear when my bishop gave us, members of his deacon council, his admonition that "if I ever hear of a deacon being divorced by his wife because he was spending too much time on his diaconate activities, and not enough time on his marital obligations, [he] would be highly upset!"

Yet marriage and Holy Orders must not be seen as competing calls—one *or* the other. Instead, the vocations must be collaborative to be viable and make Christ's presence known in the everyday world. It must be exercised in the world in which both Christians and non-Christians are to be found,

---

Conference of Catholic Bishops 2018-2019. The Center for Applied Research in the Apostolate. Page 10.

where the deacon, from his personal and intimate experiences in interacting with another person, his wife, in the truest sense of loving that person, can apply those experiences to those he serves in a way that an unmarried, celibate man cannot.

Thus the Holy Spirit, through the successors to the apostles, awakened them to the reality that whether in the celibate or the married state the man ordained must provide the model for all discipleship to be lived. And if His wishes are to be fulfilled, the married and the celibate clergy must undertake this mandated task given them at their ordination in a holistic approach.

The challenge in terms of the restored diaconate is why do we resist or overlook the synergistic effects that arise from the graces distinctly conferred on a man called to serve his Lord by living the ***dual vocations*** of a sacramental marriage and the Sacrament of Holy Orders? Recognizing this unique charism as a sacramental means of demonstrating sacrificial love to both his human and spiritual bride demonstrates living out the Lord's new commandment of love.

Would it not better show the world that both ways (the married state and the celibate state) while distinct are not different means for showing what it means to be a disciple? This would show that both ways of following Christ can be a key offering of oneself to another. This offering can be made through the sacrifice of the self to another through marriage to His Bride (Sacramental marriage) and/or the Church (through the clerical state). This is an effect, that in whichever state of life one commits to living, can only be strengthened, not diminished, through the distinct sacramental graces given to a man in the sacraments of marriage **and** (not only or) Holy Orders.

Challenge 2: The Means by which the Vocation of Deacon is Recognized

One of the challenges facing the Church with the restoration of the Order of Deacon is recognizing this "new" diaconate. These are practices related to the restored diaconate in terms of title and dress that could lead to the ***de facto*** creation of a ***fourth*** order in the Sacrament of Holy Orders. Whereas there are three grades, bishop, priest, and deacon, by its practices, the Church is inadvertently recognizing ***four***: bishop, priest, ***transitional*** deacon, and ***permanent*** deacon. This is a distinction I contend that is neither envisioned nor considered by the fathers of VCII in their decision to restore the order to its proper and permanent place in the hierarchy.

Beginning with the title, in my thirty plus years as a deacon, I have witnessed those men ordained to serve Him and His

Church referred to as "Reverend Mister," then as "Mister," leading to the designation that he was a "lay" deacon and now a "Deacon." The question this poses is as follows: Why is it that men ordained as deacon, as a step to their ordination to the priesthood, have been and still are referred to as "Reverend Mister," while men ordained as deacon, as their proper and permanent vocation, are not? Now, while recognizing the Church's absolute prerogative to do so, one would ask another question: What is the rationale for creating a public (if not official) differentiation within the Order of Deacon? It's the *same order*, the *same* ordination rite; the *same* promises made (with the exception of the commitment to celibacy for the first group and only for those of the second group who are not married)? A brother deacon, whose wife died and was accepted for ordination to the priesthood, can make my point. With the letter accepting him into priestly formation, he was now referred to as "Reverend Mister" as opposed to "Deacon." One would ask, "What caused the change in title for a man who was still the same deacon before as he was after his acceptance for ordination to the priesthood?" Although not of ontological significance, it is of ecclesiastical and sacramental significance. What message does that distinction send to the Church—both clergy and lay—as to the understanding of not only the Order of Deacon, but of the Sacrament of Holy Orders? Once more, recognizing the absolute right of the Church to make the distinction, one must ask another question: What benefit (and I can see none) is it that comes from creating the distinction? If there is a benefit, does that benefit outweigh the consequences of that distinction?

Does it not, for all practical purposes, portray in practice that the Sacrament of Holy Orders consists of not three grades but four? Does that practice, in terms of title distinction, while (albeit) legitimate, help or hinder the quest to determine **who** the deacon is? For although the distinction in terms of the **man's** vocational objective is real (one to the priesthood, the other to diaconal service), I posit that the distinction in terms of the ***Order of Deacon is not***. The challenge is one of consistency, emphasizing rather than minimizing the oneness of the order rather than the distinctness of the two calls that the ordained deacon is, or will be committed to, whether that call be to the priesthood or the diaconate.

After all, sacramentally, a deacon is a deacon. Does referring to him as "Reverend Mister" or "Deacon" help or hinder the recognition of that reality? Thus, the simple (albeit in the present Church culture, an emotional) solution would be that all deacons are referred to by one title—whether that be "Reverend Mister" or "Deacon." The benefit (and yes, the cost) is the elimination of the public emphasis on distinction, which is determined solely by the man's ultimate calling. By doing so, it will emphasize the oneness of the order. This is an effort that would be most beneficial to catechizing both clergy and laity as to not only **who** the deacon is but also **what** a deacon does.

Now, although the question of title is one of an ecclesiastic nature, continuing with the initiative as to how to publicly recognize the deacon, there is the question of attire. Again, from my experiences, this appears to be an even more emotional subject among deacons than their title. This focus on attire covers both that worn liturgically and pastorally. And again, as in the case of title, the determination of what a deacon wears, whether serving liturgically or pastorally, is recognized as being the sole discretion of the Church, a discretion that rests exclusively with the bishop.

In terms of liturgical dress, the Church has, for example, become clearer as to its recognition that the dalmatic (as opposed to the Alb and stole) is the normal dress for a deacon (whatever his focus, eventual priesthood of diaconate) when assisting at mass. Yet in terms of other liturgical functions, the distinction of the attire worn by the two, for the most part, is striking. For example, deacons aspiring to the priesthood, when performing liturgical functions such as assisting with the distribution of communion, are normally vested in a cassock, surplice, stole, and collar. The deacon, living his true vocation, is normally not. He is normally found vested in an Alb and a stole. Now, although both options are valid and appropriate for the deacon, when both "types" of deacon appear publicly in choir, the distinction in dress, once again, makes manifest to both the clergy and laity a confusion between the two. This results in genuine queries, particularly by the laity, as to why they are dressed differently. This is also the case when called upon to serve as a master of ceremonies for a liturgical function, instructed to vest in a cassock and surplice without a collar, while working alongside seminarians, who, while also vested in a cassock and surplice, are wearing a collar. Now, as pointed out earlier by my experience as a marine officer, when officers, though not "forbidden" from carrying a "swagger stick" (a long-time tradition), were challenged that "if one felt the need to carry on to do their job, then carry one." Needless to say, no one did. The same is true for liturgical dress, here the collar. I would offer a similar challenge to my brother deacons (starting with me): if a deacon feels he needs to wear a collar to serve his Lord, His Church, his parish, his bishop, then he needs to reevaluate his vocation as a deacon.

However, the issue of consistency raises its head, particularly in terms of public recognition of the **oneness** of the Order of Deacon. The policy regarding collars, at least within a particular diocese, ought to be consistent for both. Either all deacons wear collars (with whatever restrictions a bishop chooses to impose) or all do not. This is a confusion that is shown to exist, at least within the dioceses of the United States. A review of the topic in the literature on this subject showed that the policy within dioceses vary widely on this subject[34]. The trend seems to indicate a bare majority of dioceses favored deacons not aspiring to the priesthood wearing the collar. Yet again from my perspective, a collar is not essential for effective diakonia to be functional in terms of coming to an understanding of who the (restored) diaconate is. It is, after all, not a matter of sacramental or ecclesiastical theology. Yet again, it is a matter of due justice to the Order of Deacon. Put differently, the question posed is a simple one: Is it appropriate for the deacon functioning as the servant he was ordained to be, albeit while aspiring to the priesthood, to have the ability (right) to wear the collar, and inappropriate for the deacon ordained to service, who is also functioning as the servant he was ordained to be? This is a question that caused one bishop to ask me, "Nick, why are deacons so adamant about the collar?" My answer was, "Bishop,

---

[34] A good review of this topic can be fund in Deacon Greg Kandra's blog in the *Deacon's Bench,* where he points out that "US Bishops do not want a national law on this issue, because that would tie the local diocesan bishop's hands." He goes on to state that "probably by far the most common practice is that deacons may wear collars on an 'ad hoc' basis with the bishop's permission."

we don't want to be told we can't. We want to be able to exercise our discretion as our particular ministries dictate as to whether or not we ought or ought not."

Again, I believe we must look at the "benefits" of deacons, whether designated transitional or permanent wearing of the same attire, for example, whether cassock, surplus and collar or Alb and stole, whether they be liturgical or pastoral. We can compare these "benefits" to the "costs." Specifically, this can be done in terms of not only emphasizing the oneness of the Order of Deacon, but in who the deacon is. Put differently, how does the decision to emphasize the separation/distinction of the two compare in terms of the consequences associated with that decision to put an emphasis on the sameness/commonality of the order?

Challenge 3: Rethinking the Church's Approach to the Functioning of the Restored Diaconate

The Order of Deacon has one purpose: to confer on men the sacramental graces necessary to enable them to do for others **_sacramentally,_** what Jesus, from the beginning of His public ministry, has been doing for us. Doing so, however, in a sacramentally distinct way makes Christ, the perfect servant, present to others through their acting **_in persona Christi servitus._**

This is a task made more difficult by the Latin Rite experiences over the last millennium of suppressing the diaconate from what it was intended to be and making it a mere stepping stone to the priesthood. This proclivity can be seen in the implicit attempts to still define the diaconate from the perspective of that tradition, hence blurring the historical experiences that led to VCII to not only consider the viability of restoring the diaconate to its proper and permanent place, but recommend that it be so.[35]

Thus, in the assignment and tasking of the restored diaconate, we find the model in existence prior to its restoration. The newly ordained deacon is assigned (as is a priest) to a specific parish where he is tasked in way similar to that of a newly assigned priest. Put differently, the deacon (as in the old model) is assigned to a parish to be a generalist in terms of the duties assigned. This is a model that works well for the priest, who finds his primary ministry confined (in a loose sense *intra*-parish focused) to the parish and has his purpose being the sacramental and pastoral needs of the parishioners

---

[35] Which, according to Osborne, resulted in "one of the five major conciliar changes in [the Church's understanding of] ministry (pg. 7). This, Collins notes, has caused "deacons of today reflect at times on the fact that they are the first innovation in the ministerial order of the historical churches for 500 years" (pg. 143).

registered in the parish.[36]

However, the deacon, by the nature and objective of his ministry, finds his focus taking an *extra*-parish focus, one which emphasizes the community, workplace, and marketplace where he lives. This emphasis can better help the bishop (and, obviously, in a more limited way, the pastor of the parish to which he is assigned) to achieve his determined mandate, which calls for him to minister to all those people who reside within the diocesan boundaries and are in need of ecumenical support.[37]

Now, I have learned that a deacon *needs* an altar. For it is from the altar where he not only obtains from the Eucharist the sacramental graces he needs to serve those people but at the same time brings back to that same altar the petitions of those same people. These are petitions that will then be offered to the Father, along with that of the Son, at the Mass through the words and actions of the priest celebrant. That need for an altar

---

[36] Yet what we should be looking to is not models of the past for determining not only what the present diaconate should be, thus creating a model that will at best impede the restored diaconate to effectively carry out the vision for which the fathers at VCII saw the need to be, but to the present environment in which the church finds itself faced with carrying out the Lord's mandate to serve those in need where they are.

[37] See Figure 3 above.

obviously is not the case with a priest. He (through the faculties given him at his priestly ordination) ***brings his altar with him wherever he may be.*** This is not the case with a deacon. Therefore, it is imperative that he be assigned to a parish to have that altar available to him in an ***official*** way.[38]

However, that does not mean, nor should it limit, his official assignment(s) (whatever it/they may be) to the parish. If indeed he is ordained to serve the bishop (as stressed in the ordination rite), then to be consistent, his normal ***diaconal*** (not necessarily organizational) assignment should be a diocesan, ***not*** a parish assignment, for example, assignment to the Family Life Office, the Tribunal, the Finance Office, or Catholic Charities, to name a few. Such assignments would be truly diaconal ministries carried out in the bishop's name—the reason for his ordination. Doing so does not (nor should it) take away from his availability to assist the pastor of the parish to which he is assigned (as, in a loosely given analogy, the priest living in residence at a parish who has an assignment outside of that parish).

Taking this perspective will lead to the recognition that for the diocesan assignment to be effective, deacons should be

---

[38] This applies in an even more critical sense to those deacons who are retired and no longer are assigned to a parish.

trained to be more than generalists. Isn't that what the bishop does with his priests, who are normally looked on as generalists, whom he wishes to serve him in a specific way (e.g., working on the Tribunal)? Why not (maybe not always with the same degree of in-depth training) do the same for deacons? The one advantage a deacon normally brings is his secular expertise. This experience should be taken into account in his assignment upon ordination. Taking such an approach would then pose the following question: In which role, the diocesan assignment or parish assignment, would the deacon be better able to serve the bishop in the manner stressed at his ordination?[39]

Challenge 4: Deacon Selection

Two things stood out for me when attending the Deacon Congress in New Orleans, and both came about from attending a presentation on the CARA findings from a recent survey sent out to deacons nationwide. The first was that more and more dioceses in the United States have established or are in the process of establishing retirement policies for deacons. And although the policies range widely as to the specifics, the

---

[39] For a much more reasoned and structured understanding of the point, see McKnight part 4, chapters 8 and 9.

one that is constant is a consensus as to the age of retirement being seventy-five. This is a fact, in and of itself, that is not necessarily noteworthy. However, the second thing brought to light by the survey was that the average age of men ordained to the diaconate in the United States was fifty-eight, and the average age for ordaining men in Europe was forty-six.[40]

Think of the implications of those two factors and the significant impact they have on active diaconal ministry. Using those statistics, we find that the average active ministry in the United States is seventeen years, whereas using the same criteria, the average active ministry of a deacon in Europe would be twenty-nine years—a difference of some twelve years of effective diaconal service.

Now, that difference, albeit notional, poses two questions. Why is the diaconal population significantly younger in Europe than it is in the United States? What impact does that have on the functioning of those ordained to the Order of Deacon?"

In terms of the first question, I believe it has to do with the perception of the restored diaconate in the United States. In the first place, the perception of both the man who feels he is called to serve His Lord and His Church as an ordained deacon

---

[40] See the latest CARA report presented at the recent Deacon Congress in New Orleans.

and the Church that assesses that call in terms of genuineness, expectation, and commitment appear to be the same. Both perspectives look to the diaconate, based on developing experiences with the restored diaconate, as a "second calling." The implication being that the man, in and through his "first calling," whether that be identified with the career/profession he has participated in during his professional life *or* his response to his call to the married life is *now* ready to enter into this "secondary" way of life as a deacon.

Thus, both the man and the Church tend to gravitate to those who are either well along in their "first" career as a professional or their "first calling" to the matrimonial state. In both cases, they have thus "proven" themselves to be successful at what they had committed to do. Only now are they deemed to be ready of beginning a "new" journey. This is what some would call a "second" journey, one in which the commitment, when compared with that of a priest (or a male or female religious), is not as great in terms of what is expected on the part of both the man and the Church. This is a perception that in many ways perpetuates the "myth" of the "part-time" deacon.

Then, there is the reality that over 90% of the men approaching their bishop for consideration to be ordained deacons are married and have a well-established/mature family. One might ponder the question as to whether that is an innate proclivity or one officially merely encouraged. This is a policy giving the perception that the man should wait until his family has grown up before he applies, giving the rationale that it would be "too much" of a burden for the married man in training, as well as the man ordained deacon to carry out his functions, with small children. Again, from personal experience and the experience of married couples, I have found that to be just the opposite. Almost without exception, if asked, deacons and their wives would say it is harder to cope with grown children than it is with small children. Their response would point out, particularly in the preparation for and functioning as a deacon, that it is/was easier when the children were little: no soccer practices and games; no after school band practices and performances; no after school extracurricular activities, much of which, particularly for families with multiple children, are not held at the same place at the same time. All of these are activities to which parents are committed to seeing their children get there and back. Yet men with small children, for whom the "logistics" are nowhere near as complex or time consuming, for the most part, are either explicitly or implicitly discouraged from applying for ordination to the diaconate until their children are "grown."

Both perceptions can only result in an "older" diaconate. The effect is that any diaconal support received by a pastor is considered as "pure profit," whether it be for seventeen or twenty-nine years. The implication is that while the deacon's service is both recognized and appreciated, the parish, in terms of serving its parishioners, whether sacramentally or pastorally, that service would continue, thus causing more work for the priests without the presence of deacons.

Yet in objective terms, an older diaconate, when faced with a mandatory retirement cap, can only cause the Church to lose the advantage (and availability) of the ordained deacon's expertise in terms of service to the Church, bishop, and parish.

This reality should cause the bishop to pause in terms of how he will select, form, and assign his deacons. Why would the bishop want to "take away" a man from diaconal service for any length of time to provide the training necessary to assign the deacon to a diocesan role, for example, whether in support of the Family Life Office, the Tribunal, or Catholic Charities? This lack of a deacon presence at the diocesan level is a practice that has impacted the intended relationship that should exist between a bishop and his deacons.

Challenge 5: Permanent: Description rather than Designation

The *Catechism of the Catholic Church* makes explicit the fact that the deacon is "***not*** ordained to the priesthood but to service."[41] This is a distinction that was stressed by Pope Benedict XVI when he authorized the change to the *Catechism* to point out that it was the man ordained a priest, ***not*** the man ordained to the diaconate, who received a sacerdotal character at his ordination.

The *Catechism*, although it does differentiate the priest and the deacon, however, makes ***no*** distinction in its description of the ordained deacon; whether the deacon is ordained to ***the vocation by which he was called to serve Christ*** or ordained in anticipation of his being ordained a priest, ***the vocation by which he was called to serve Christ***. It is interesting to note that both the deacon and the priest find their distinct ministries begin, derive from, and are sustained by the altar, albeit each in a significantly different way. This is a distinction that better defines the particular way that Christ is asking them to serve Him. It allows us to see the essential need for collaboration and cooperation between the priest and the deacon in carrying out

---

[41] CCC Article 1569

the Lord's mandate. For the priest, in living his vocation, and who does so most perfectly *at* the altar, which, because of his priesthood, is to be found wherever he is—a reality made manifest by the Lord at the Last Supper. However, the deacon, while living his vocation by "waiting the table," lives that vocation most perfectly *away* from the altar, from which his diaconal effectiveness is derived as again, made manifest by the Lord at the Last Supper, who left the table to serve those found away from the altar.

Again, whether we look to the criteria set forth in the *Catechism* as to what ordination to the diaconate means or to the actions of the Lord in his diaconal activities at the Last Supper, we find no distinction in terms of who a deacon is, why a deacon is ordained, and what a deacon is called to do. Hence, when it comes to recognizing *a deacon*, it must be recognized that he should not only *serve Our Lord sacramentally,* but make Christ the Servant's presence known through the conferral of Holy Orders. In short, *his essence is service.* This is a service that is to be undertaken in a sacramental and specific way.

So, this is true that whether a man is ordained a deacon as his chosen vocation or in anticipation for entering the priesthood does not (nor should it) differentiate one from the other. As long as *both* hold the Order of Deacon, both have *one* mandate; *one* objective; and *one* reason for existence: ***diakonia.***

Christ, through His actions at the Last Supper demonstrated the diaconate is a true vocation oriented to service. The question is why then ordain a man whose "true" vocation was the priesthood to the Order of Deacon? I believe it was for a specific, ecclesial, and ontological reason: to expose the man to be ordained to the priesthood to the reality that the perfect sacrifice, is a ***sacrifice of service.*** It is a ***service*** to and for others that Jesus exercised most perfectly in and through His sacrifice of the cross. It is a ***service*** He wanted His priests to realize through their living their experience as an ordained deacon. They can see that they will always be a ***servant set apart through their ordination.*** This is a reality which He wants his priests to always remember, even if they go on to be bishops, that they will **always** be **His servant**, ***always*** be **His deacon**, serving Him in the particular way He chooses for them to do so.

Challenge 6: Restoration of the Bishop–Deacon Relationship

The Catechism of the Catholic Church (Art 1569), referring back to Hippolytus, points out that "at an ordination to the diaconate only the bishop lays hands on the candidate, thus signifying the deacon's special attachment to the bishop in his tasks of 'diakonia.'" Hippolytus points out that this is "...to serve the bishop and fulfill the bishop's command," which is "to acquaint the bishop with such matters as are needful..."[42]

Since the suppression of the diaconate as a viable ministry in the Latin Church, the bishop–deacon relationship has become customarily liturgical in nature, that is, the deacon's relationship with the bishop is normally seen to exist when he is assisting the bishop in celebrating Mass. I contend this has not been the preferred or expected way that the relationship between the deacon and bishop was meant to be. The relationship envisioned by the Council and Pope Saint Paul VI was different. They recognized there was a need for the official, sacramental Church to be made present where people were, not merely where they worshiped. This was to enable the bishop, through the experiences of, and his interactions with his deacons, to have a better pulse on his flock. Otherwise, would not then those men ordained deacons as a transitional step to the priesthood in their diaconate serve this liturgical purpose? Indeed, the deacon ordained for service gains the graces to sustain him in his diaconal efforts from the Eucharist given to him **at the** altar. These are the graces which he then takes from the altar to strengthen him in his service to others. The deacon

---

[42] Hippolytus: *The Apostolic Tradition*

transitionally ordained, however, takes from his service at the altar the graces that will strengthen him in his commitment and to prepare him for his ordination to the priesthood. These are experiences that will enable him to commit to become proficient with the requirements for offering the Sacrifice of the Mass. Then when ordained a priest, he can continue to offer that one, perfect sacrifice as Christ, the *servant*, offered from His Cross. Thus, although the deacon ordained for permanent service is given the graces to become more proficient in his *pastoral* activities, the deacon ordained in transition to the priesthood is given the graces that enable him to function (albeit for a limited period) as a servant to others, as well as become more proficient in his eventual *sacerdotal* activities.

It is precisely because of those relationships, determined by the distinct way and place the bishop and the deacon are called upon to live their distinct vocations, that we find the answer as to why the diaconate was restored: to establish a dynamic and synergistic relationship between the bishop and his deacon(s) as it relates to his flock. The flock among which the deacon lives his vocation.

Yet for the most part, we find, even after some fifty years of having the restored diaconate, the "traditional" relationship of the bishop and the deacon, in terms of ecclesiastical matters, is still a relationship that is exercised *through the priest* (both to and from the one to the other). Thus, the bishop–deacon relationship that was originally intended and publicly evinced at the deacon's ordination, where the bishop–deacon relationship was defined, is not evidenced. Despite its original intent, it is a relationship found to be exercised in a merely communal, usually at a social level, of interaction. This is reinforced by the normal assigning of a deacon exclusively to a parish, whereby the intended bishop–deacon relationship has become, for all practical purposes, a priest–deacon relationship.

Returning to the fact that the deacon needs an altar, assignment to a parish is not only a functional but an essential way to ensure that happens. However, if the effectiveness of the restored diaconate in achieving the objectives that caused its restoration is to be realized, the assignment of a deacon **exclusively** to a parish needs to be reevaluated. Therefore, if the deacon is to be the eyes and ears of the bishop in pastoral matters affecting the bishop's "sheep," then the assignment of a deacon to a diocesan ministry as his primary focus must be given serious consideration.[43] For in doing so, the deacon, in living a diocesan focused vocation, is placed in a situation that makes the bishop–deacon relationship not only more realistic,

---

[43] See McKnight's perspective as to the specific ways this can take place in his Chapter 8.

but more effective. Taking this approach would not only make the deacon, but the bishop, more capable of doing the will of the One who called each to his distinct vocation.

Challenge 7: Ritual Reinforcement of the Deacon's Commitment to His Vocation

One of the things that sets Catholics apart in terms of their religious commitment and practice is that they are primarily *sacramental* people. They look to the sacraments instituted by Jesus, as the primary means for attaining the specific graces they need to live out their particular call to discipleship. Yet the sacramental graces offered have, as a "condition," a commitment on the part of the recipient to live that particular sacrament as Christ intends for it to be lived. Take, for example, the Sacrament of Reconciliation. One significant condition is a commitment on the part of the penitent to amend their ways of living their discipleship. However, by God's will, three of the seven sacraments were instituted by Christ as a means for giving one the graces needed to live their discipleship and to do so in a way that the commitment asked of the recipient is not merely a lifelong commitment but an eternal one.

And one of the key elements in recognizing a Catholic's

commitment to the discipleship called for by these three sacraments, Baptism, Confirmation, and Holy Orders, is the matter of Sacred Chrism. The Chrism is first used at a person's baptism, signifying not only his relationship with, but his commitment to, the Anointed One. This is a commitment to living their discipleship in whatever form it is that Christ determines it to be so that it makes His Presence known to the world in which they live. The *same* Chrism is used at a person's Confirmation, signifying the sealing of that person's commitment to a fuller relationship with Christ. This is a commitment strengthened by an increase of the gifts of the Holy Spirit, which are first bestowed at the person's baptism. The *same* Chrism is used in the Sacrament of Holy Orders when conferring the Order of Episcopate on a man who has been called to be a successor to the apostles, here by anointing his *head.* It is a sign of his responsibility to be a shepherd to the flock entrusted to him by exposing them, teaching them, and guiding them to the truths contained in the Deposit of Faith. These are truths to which the bishop is committed to hold and protect. It is the *same* Chrism used when conferring the Order of Priesthood on a man who has been called to offer the Sacrifice of the Mass, to symbolize the strengthening of his vocation to sacrifice, here by anointing his *hands.* Yet it is *not* used when it comes to the ordination of a man called to the

Order of Deacon. Is not a deacon called to a vocation of service to the others in the person of the *same Anointed One*? Would not a deacon, as it is deemed necessary for a bishop or a priest, also need the symbolic strengthening of his vocation by the use of the same Sacred Chrism, albeit in a way unlike the one in which a bishop and a priest were at their ordination?

Looking at the institution of the Sacrament of Holy Orders at the Last Supper, one would ask the following: What better way to *symbolically* strengthen the deacon's vocational commitment than by following the example of the Anointed One in the washing of His apostles' feet, here then anointing the deacon's *feet*?[44] The feet will carry him out into the marketplace, the workplace, and the community, places he is called to live his vocation of serving the Anointed One in those who were created in His image and likeness. This is a symbol of which is made manifest each year at the Mass of the Lord's Supper, when the celebrant, whether bishop or priest, is publicly reminded by his actions that he was *first* a deacon, a servant of and for Christ, *before* he was a priest or bishop. This is a point made so clear by Pope Francis, when washing the feet of parishioners, turned his stole to that of *a deacon*.

---

[44] For was it not in the act of having His feet anointed that He proclaimed that we will "always have the poor," the population that is the main focus of the diaconia?

Think about it. What are the first words heard by a newly ordained deacon? "Receive the Gospel, whose herald you are. Believe what you read; teach what you believe; and *live what you teach*" (emphasis added). In effect, isn't the ordaining bishop saying, "I, as a successor to the apostles, commissioned as they were by the Lord to proclaim the Good News to all the world, am ordaining you to support me in carrying out my commission. But you do so not where I, nor my priests normally do, but where you are normally found. In the neighborhood where you *live,* in the workplace where you earn your *living,* and in the shopping center where you obtain your *life's* necessities"? In doing so, would not the deacon fall under Paul's proclamation as to "how beautiful are the *feet* (emphasis added) of those who preach the Good News" (Rom 10:14-17).

Then, there is the traditional and symbolic commitment of priests to renew annually their priestly commitment each time they participate in the Chrism mass. Recognizing, thanks be to God, that priests take their priestly commitment seriously, why then is there the need to renew that commitment annually? I have learned as a married man that although there is no need to do so, there is a definitive strengthening of one's steadfast commitment to the Sacrament of Marriage by renewing that covenantal vow made on one's wedding day on some regular basis, usually on a significant anniversary. This is a renewal that is of similar benefit for a man committed to his priestly vocation. The question then is as follows: If it is of benefit for a priest to do so, why then not a deacon? I had the honor of serving a bishop who would send me (and my brother deacons) a note of thanksgiving on the anniversary of our ordination. In sharing that experience with my brother deacons, it was felt to be a unanimous sense of not only acceptance, but belonging. And more so, it gave us a renewed sense of commitment to serving him.

Why should there not then, in a similar sense to that called for a priest, be a renewal of a man's commitment to his diaconal vocation? For if there is a benefit for a priest to do so, one would think the same benefit would be experienced by a deacon doing so. And what better liturgical symbolism for doing so would be than at the Mass of the Lord's Supper—already heavy in diaconal symbolism by the washing of the feet. Now, the gathering of all deacons at the cathedral to do so, while not impossible, is certainly impractical. For where there is only one Chrism mass, to which a priest can give his undivided attention, the Mass of the Lord's Supper is celebrated at all the parishes in the diocese. It is a liturgy that the deacons assigned to those parishes should assist at. So how can this annual commitment of a deacon to his diaconal vocation be publicly offered?

One possible way would be that proposed by Deacon Ditewig. He proposes a way that brings with it many advantages as to both the availability of both the deacons and their bishop:[45] is that the bishop gathers his deacons together annually on December 26, the feast of Saint Stephen, to recognize his deacons in a public way. This is something I and my brother deacons assigned to our parish did; we gathered together on that day and assisted at the mass celebrated by our pastor, at which we were publicly recognized.

The sign, however, in whatever forum would be a sign to both deacons and the community as to the reality of the diaconate. On the one hand, it would not only recognize, but encourage, vocations to the diaconate. On the other hand, it would incentivize the laity to recognize that through their baptism, they too are called to serve their brothers and sisters, each in their own way. The cost, in terms of the logistics involved in an annual recommitment of deacons to their vocation, would be insignificant when measured against the benefits to both the deacons and laity.

---

[45] Ditewig, *The Emerging Diaconate*, pg. 102.

Conclusion

Who is the deacon? From my experiences, as well as my research and what I have proposed above, I can say with a great degree of confidence that the deacon is nothing other than **Christ the Servant made sacramentally present to the world in which he lives his vocation**.

The deacon is the one who, by living among, rather than apart from the "sheep," gains an empirical rather than notional sense of *how* the sheep "smell, "as well as *what* the sheep require. These experiences will enable deacons, thanks to their presence among them, to live their vocation as a viable and fruitful enabler of their flock. The flock is entrusted to those who have been and will continue to be called to succeed the apostles as their shepherds. The bishops are called to be responsible for their particular sheepfold, which is entrusted to them by their ordination to the episcopate. What better way for them to do so then by not only enabling, but encouraging, the men called by him to live their vocation as a deacon, to make aware to him, in a fraternal way, those services his flock needs?

By accepting the deacon for who he is—Christ the Servant sacramentalized—rather than by what he can or cannot do, then what the deacon does or does not do as a deacon will not be the driving factor as to his existence. Why? Because whatever the deacon does, in living his vocation, would be done *for* Christ, *through* Christ, and *to* Christ in whoever and wherever it is his vocation takes him.

Therefore, for the deacon to be considered effective, in terms of who the Lord called him to be, his diakonia can only be evaluated by its being focused, related, and responsive to the particular "smell" of the sheep that make up the flock entrusted to the bishop whom the deacon, in obedience, was called to serve. This obedience, however, if it is to be an effective means of making present to the world a viable diaconate, cannot be imposed only encouraged. It must be an obedience that cannot be merely reactive: it must be proactive. In other words, it is an obedience that creates a synergistic relationship between the bishop and deacon that translates into a dynamic rather than static diakonia. Which then poses another question: How can such a service be effective?

This is a question that still needs an answer, even after fifty years of the Church's experiences with the restored diaconate. Is it a diaconate that is encouraged to be proactive in making Christ the Servant known to the "sheep?" Is it a diakonia that not only enables their particular "smells "to be experienced and responded to? This is a question that has two possible answers. One view (and I pray to be the minority view), as put to me by a brother deacon ordained before me, was that "the diaconate was a noble experiment that, because of the way it has been implemented, is ripe for failure." The other view is (I believe to be in the vast majority and to which I hold) that we need to look to the Holy Spirit's inspiration of Saint John XXIII to call a council to *"shake the Church out of her lethargy and go out to preach the Gospel, the precious gift that she had been given by Jesus Christ, to the world. [Which would require the Church to] "'update' the message so that it would resonate with the world. "46* Doing so would "better assist the Church in adapting to changes that were more rapidly taking place in the world.[47]" Once the Second Vatican Council had convened, however, to see that same Spirit inspired the council fathers to recognize that one powerful way for those objectives to be achieved, was the restoration of the diaconate to its proper and permanent place in its hierarchy.

---

[46] https://w2.vatican.va/content/john-xxiii/en/speeches/1962
[47] Ibid.

Thus, I have come to the conclusion that no better example of how Pope Saint John XXIII's objectives concerning the restored diaconate can be accomplished than for the deacon to put himself in the shoes of those servants at the Wedding Feast of Cana. It was there, when asked by our Mother Mary, to do whatever her Son asked, they responded without question, without hesitation to what He asked of them. By their ordination to the diaconate, He is asking the same thing of them, calling out to His servants: "do my will!" He asks them to do My will in a way that your diakonia brings glory to the Father. For if deacons, like the servants at Cana, do so, they too will find that through their diakonia, the particular needs of the sheep will be met.

Epilogue

[A]Pharisee in the Sanhedrin named Gamaliel, a teacher of the law, respected by all the people, stood up, ordered the men to be put outside for a short time, and said to them, "Fellow Israelites, be careful what you are about to do to these men. For if this endeavor or this activity is of human origin, it will destroy itself. But if it comes from God, you will not be able to destroy them; you may even find yourselves fighting against God." They were persuaded by him.

Acts 5: 34-39

In terms of **who** the deacon is, **are you persuaded?**

Selected Bibliography

Barnett, James M.Th. **Diaconate** A *Full and Equal Order,* The Seabury Press, NY. 1981

Cerrato, Dominic, In the Person of Christ the Servant *A Theology of the Diaconate Based on the Personalist Thought of Pope John Paul II,* St. Ephraem Press, OH. 2016

Chryssavgis, John, Remembering and Reclaiming Diakonia *The Diaconate Yesterday and Today* Holy Cross Orthodox Press, MA. 2009

Collins, John N. Diakonia, *Re-interpreting the Ancient Sources,* Oxford University Press, NY. 1990

Collins, John N., Deacons and the Church Making connections between old and new, Gracewing, Morehouse Publishing, PA. 2002

Ditewig, William T., **The Emerging Diaconate** Servant Leaders in a Servant Church, Paulist Press, NY/ NJ. 2007

Ditewig, William T., Tkacik, Michael J., Editor, **Forming Deacons** Ministers of Souls and Leaven, Paulist Press, NY/NJ. 2010

Echlin, Edward P., **The Deacon in the Church**, *Past and Future*, Alba House, NY. 1971

From the Diakonia of Christ to the Diakonia of the Apostles, International Theological Commission. 2003

Kleiber, Kenneth and Lemire, Herve, Deacons: Permanent or Passing *An Update on the Permanent Diaconate of the Catholic Church in the United States*, Richelieu Court Aspen Heights, Slingerlands, NY. 1982

McCaslin, Patrick and Lawler, Michael G., **Sacrament of Service**, *A Vision of the Permanent Diaconate Today*, Paulist Press, NY/NJ. 1986

McKnight, W. Shawn, <u>Understanding the Diaconate</u> *Historical, Theological, and Sociological Foundations*, The Catholic University Press of America, Washington DC, 2018.

Muller, Gerhard, <u>Priesthood and Diaconate</u>, Ignatius Press, CA. 2002

Osborne, Kenan B., <u>The Permanent Diaconate</u> *Its History and Place in the Sacraments of Orders*, Paulist Press, NY/NJ. 2006

Petrolino, Enzo, Editor, <u>Compendium on the Diaconate</u> *A Resource for the Formation, Ministry, and Life of the Permanent Deacon*, Libreria Editrice, United States Conference of Catholic Bishops, Washington DC May. 2015

Plater, Osmonde, <u>Many Servants</u>, *An Introduction to Deacons*, Cowley Publications, MA. 1991

Renken, John Anthony, The Deacon in Vatican Council II *A Consideration of the Conciliar Teaching in View of the Historical Development of the Office* (Dissertatio Ad Lauream Roma). 1981

Strauch, Alexander, **The New Testament Deacon** *Minister of Mercy*, Lewis and Roth Publishers, CO. 1992

Ziegler, John J., **Let Them Anoint the Sick**, The Liturgical Press, MN. 1987